DIARY 2006
EXPLORING BRITAIN

FRANCES LINCOLN

Frances Lincoln Limited
4 Torriano Mews
Torriano Avenue
London NW5 2RZ
www.franceslincoln.com

National Railway Museum Diary 2006
Copyright © Frances Lincoln Limited 2005

Text and illustrations copyright © National Railway Museum, York/ Science & Society Picture Library, London 2005.
Science & Society Picture Library represents the collections of the National Railway Museum in York.
www.scienceandsociety.co.uk

Astronomical information reproduced, with permission, from data supplied by HM Nautical Almanac Office, copyright © Council for the Central Laboratory of the Research Councils.

All rights reserved. No part of this publication may be reproduced, stored in a retrieval system or transmitted, in any form, or by any means, electronic, mechanical, photocopying, recording or otherwise, without either prior permission in writing from the publishers or a licence permitting restricted copying. In the United Kingdom such licences are issued by the Copyright Licensing Agency, 90 Tottenham Court Road, London W1T 4LP.

British Library cataloguing-in-publication data
A catalogue record for this book is available from the British Library

ISBN 0-7112-2511-7
Printed in China
First Frances Lincoln edition 2005

FRONT COVER
A Cheshire Lines Railway poster of 1935 advertising 'The pleasure route to Southport' in Merseyside.

BACK COVER
A poster by Reg Lander produced by BR to promote rail travel to the seaside resort of Paignton in South Devon.

TITLE PAGE
A GWR poster by Edward McKnight Kauffer advertising 'Great Western to Devon's moors'.

OPPOSITE INTRODUCTION
A BR (Eastern Region) poster of the 1950s by Myers, which appeared with the slogan 'Faster all along the line by British Railways'.

VISITORS' INFORMATION

National Railway Museum
Leeman Road
York, YO26 4XJ

Telephone: 01904 621261
Fax: 01904 611112
e-mail: nrm@nmsi.ac.uk
website: www.nrm.org.uk

24 hour recorded information line: 01904 686286

Admission free

Open
Daily: 10 am to 6 pm
Closed: 24th, 25th & 26th December

Gift Shop
The gift shop is open daily and sells a selection of souvenirs, gifts, videos and books.

Restaurants
The Brief Encounter restaurant in the Station Hall, serving full meals or light snacks, and the Signal Box café in the Great Hall, serving drinks and light snacks, are both open daily.

Disabled visitors
Ramps and lifts provide access to most parts of the museum and wheelchairs may be borrowed from the entrance. There are free disabled parking bays outside the City Entrance. Support dogs are welcome.

Reference Library
The museum has an extensive collection of books, archives, photographs and pictorial works which may be viewed free of charge. The library is open Monday to Friday from 10 am to 5 pm and pre-booking is required. To make an appointment, telephone 01904 686235.

2006

JANUARY
M	T	W	T	F	S	S
						1
2	3	4	5	6	7	8
9	10	11	12	13	14	15
16	17	18	19	20	21	22
23	24	25	26	27	28	29
30	31					

FEBRUARY
M	T	W	T	F	S	S
		1	2	3	4	5
6	7	8	9	10	11	12
13	14	15	16	17	18	19
20	21	22	23	24	25	26
27	28					

MARCH
M	T	W	T	F	S	S
		1	2	3	4	5
6	7	8	9	10	11	12
13	14	15	16	17	18	19
20	21	22	23	24	25	26
27	28	29	30	31		

APRIL
M	T	W	T	F	S	S
					1	2
3	4	5	6	7	8	9
10	11	12	13	14	15	16
17	18	19	20	21	22	23
24	25	26	27	28	29	30

MAY
M	T	W	T	F	S	S
1	2	3	4	5	6	7
8	9	10	11	12	13	14
15	16	17	18	19	20	21
22	23	24	25	26	27	28
29	30	31				

JUNE
M	T	W	T	F	S	S
			1	2	3	4
5	6	7	8	9	10	11
12	13	14	15	16	17	18
19	20	21	22	23	24	25
26	27	28	29	30		

JULY
M	T	W	T	F	S	S
					1	2
3	4	5	6	7	8	9
10	11	12	13	14	15	16
17	18	19	20	21	22	23
24	25	26	27	28	29	30
31						

AUGUST
M	T	W	T	F	S	S
	1	2	3	4	5	6
7	8	9	10	11	12	13
14	15	16	17	18	19	20
21	22	23	24	25	26	27
28	29	30	31			

SEPTEMBER
M	T	W	T	F	S	S
				1	2	3
4	5	6	7	8	9	10
11	12	13	14	15	16	17
18	19	20	21	22	23	24
25	26	27	28	29	30	

OCTOBER
M	T	W	T	F	S	S
						1
2	3	4	5	6	7	8
9	10	11	12	13	14	15
16	17	18	19	20	21	22
23	24	25	26	27	28	29
30	31					

NOVEMBER
M	T	W	T	F	S	S
		1	2	3	4	5
6	7	8	9	10	11	12
13	14	15	16	17	18	19
20	21	22	23	24	25	26
27	28	29	30			

DECEMBER
M	T	W	T	F	S	S
				1	2	3
4	5	6	7	8	9	10
11	12	13	14	15	16	17
18	19	20	21	22	23	24
25	26	27	28	29	30	31

2007

JANUARY
M	T	W	T	F	S	S
1	2	3	4	5	6	7
8	9	10	11	12	13	14
15	16	17	18	19	20	21
22	23	24	25	26	27	28
29	30	31				

FEBRUARY
M	T	W	T	F	S	S
			1	2	3	4
5	6	7	8	9	10	11
12	13	14	15	16	17	18
19	20	21	22	23	24	25
26	27	28				

MARCH
M	T	W	T	F	S	S
			1	2	3	4
5	6	7	8	9	10	11
12	13	14	15	16	17	18
19	20	21	22	23	24	25
26	27	28	29	30	31	

APRIL
M	T	W	T	F	S	S
						1
2	3	4	5	6	7	8
9	10	11	12	13	14	15
16	17	18	19	20	21	22
23	24	25	26	27	28	29
30						

MAY
M	T	W	T	F	S	S
	1	2	3	4	5	6
7	8	9	10	11	12	13
14	15	16	17	18	19	20
21	22	23	24	25	26	27
28	29	30	31			

JUNE
M	T	W	T	F	S	S
				1	2	3
4	5	6	7	8	9	10
11	12	13	14	15	16	17
18	19	20	21	22	23	24
25	26	27	28	29	30	

JULY
M	T	W	T	F	S	S
						1
2	3	4	5	6	7	8
9	10	11	12	13	14	15
16	17	18	19	20	21	22
23	24	25	26	27	28	29
30	31					

AUGUST
M	T	W	T	F	S	S
		1	2	3	4	5
6	7	8	9	10	11	12
13	14	15	16	17	18	19
20	21	22	23	24	25	26
27	28	29	30	31		

SEPTEMBER
M	T	W	T	F	S	S
					1	2
3	4	5	6	7	8	9
10	11	12	13	14	15	16
17	18	19	20	21	22	23
24	25	26	27	28	29	30

OCTOBER
M	T	W	T	F	S	S
1	2	3	4	5	6	7
8	9	10	11	12	13	14
15	16	17	18	19	20	21
22	23	24	25	26	27	28
29	30	31				

NOVEMBER
M	T	W	T	F	S	S
			1	2	3	4
5	6	7	8	9	10	11
12	13	14	15	16	17	18
19	20	21	22	23	24	25
26	27	28	29	30		

DECEMBER
M	T	W	T	F	S	S
					1	2
3	4	5	6	7	8	9
10	11	12	13	14	15	16
17	18	19	20	21	22	23
24	25	26	27	28	29	30
31						

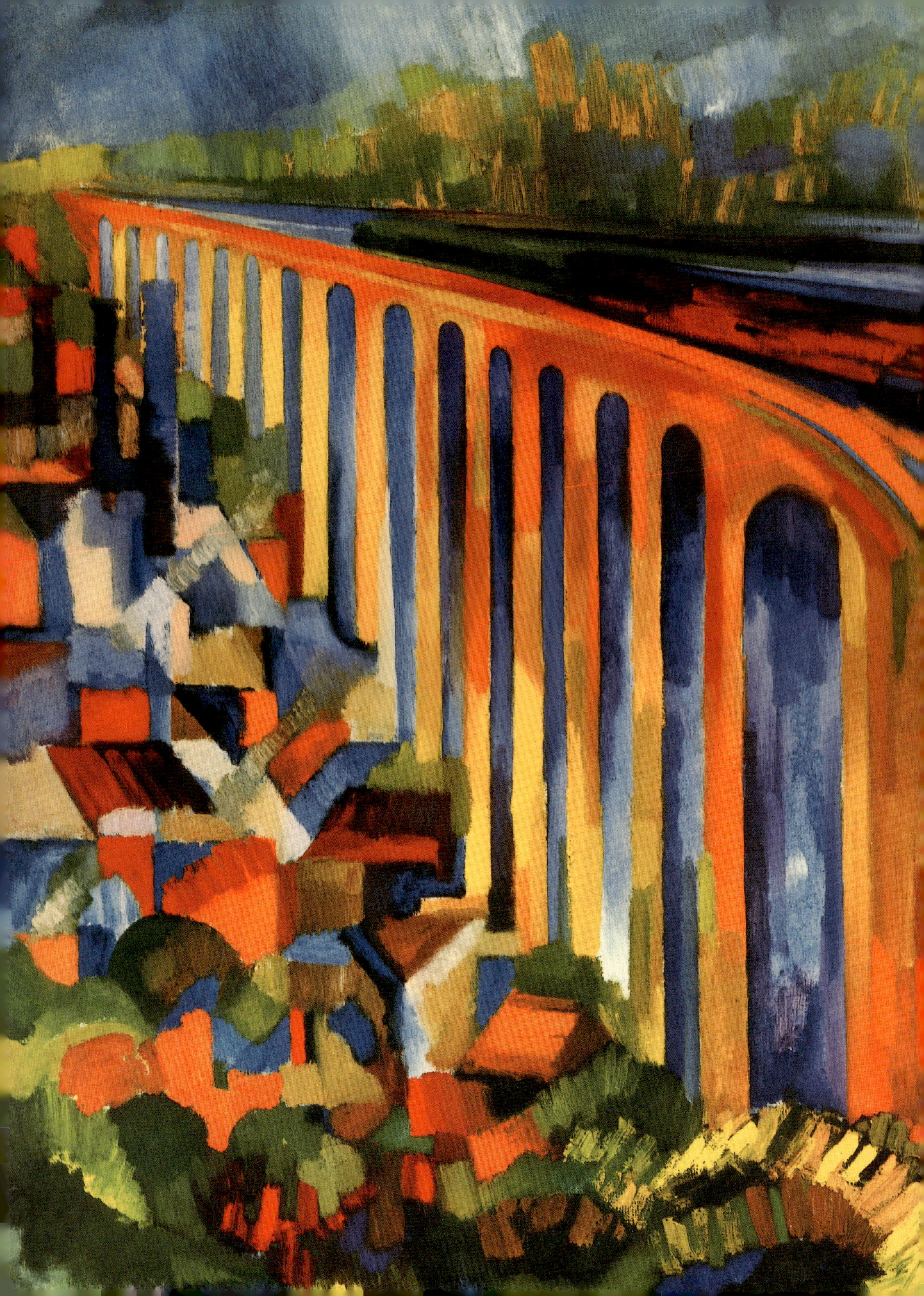

INTRODUCTION

The period between 1923 and 1947 was the heyday of the railway poster. These were the years of the so-called 'Big Four' companies – the Great Western Railway (GWR), the Southern Railway (SR), the London Midland and Scottish Railway (LMS) and the London and North Eastern Railway (LNER). Competing for passengers, the companies each produced colourful and dramatic posters featuring destinations covered by their networks. The posters relied on good design and a strong image for their appeal, and developed into a distinctive style of poster advertising.

With the creation of the British Transport Commission in 1948, the 'Big Four' companies passed into public ownership. Rail nationalization brought optimism and hope to many and this was reflected in the British Railways posters of the 1950s and 1960s, which recapture much of the fun of earlier years.

Included in this diary are a selection of posters from the 'Big Four', British Railways and other railway companies such as the London & North Western Railway (LNWR), the Cheshire Lines Railway and the Romney, Hythe and Dymchurch Railway (RHDR). They are all from the collection of 7,000 historic railway posters in the National Railway Museum in York. The museum is the largest of its kind in the world, home to a wide range of railway icons and literally millions of artefacts, from Mallard – the world's fastest steam engine – to a lock of Robert Stephenson's hair, and a vast collection of 103 locomotives and engines.

WEEK 52, 2005

DECEMBER & JANUARY

26 MONDAY
Boxing Day (St Stephen's Day)
Holiday, UK, Republic of Ireland, Canada,
USA, Australia and New Zealand
(Christmas Day observed)

27 TUESDAY
Holiday, UK, Republic of Ireland, Canada,
Australia and New Zealand
(Boxing Day observed)

28 WEDNESDAY

29 THURSDAY

30 FRIDAY

31 SATURDAY
New Year's Eve
NEW MOON

1 SUNDAY
New Year's Day

Northern Counties Hotel, *Portrush*, a poster by Gordon Nicoll advertising LMS's services to Portrush in Northern Ireland.

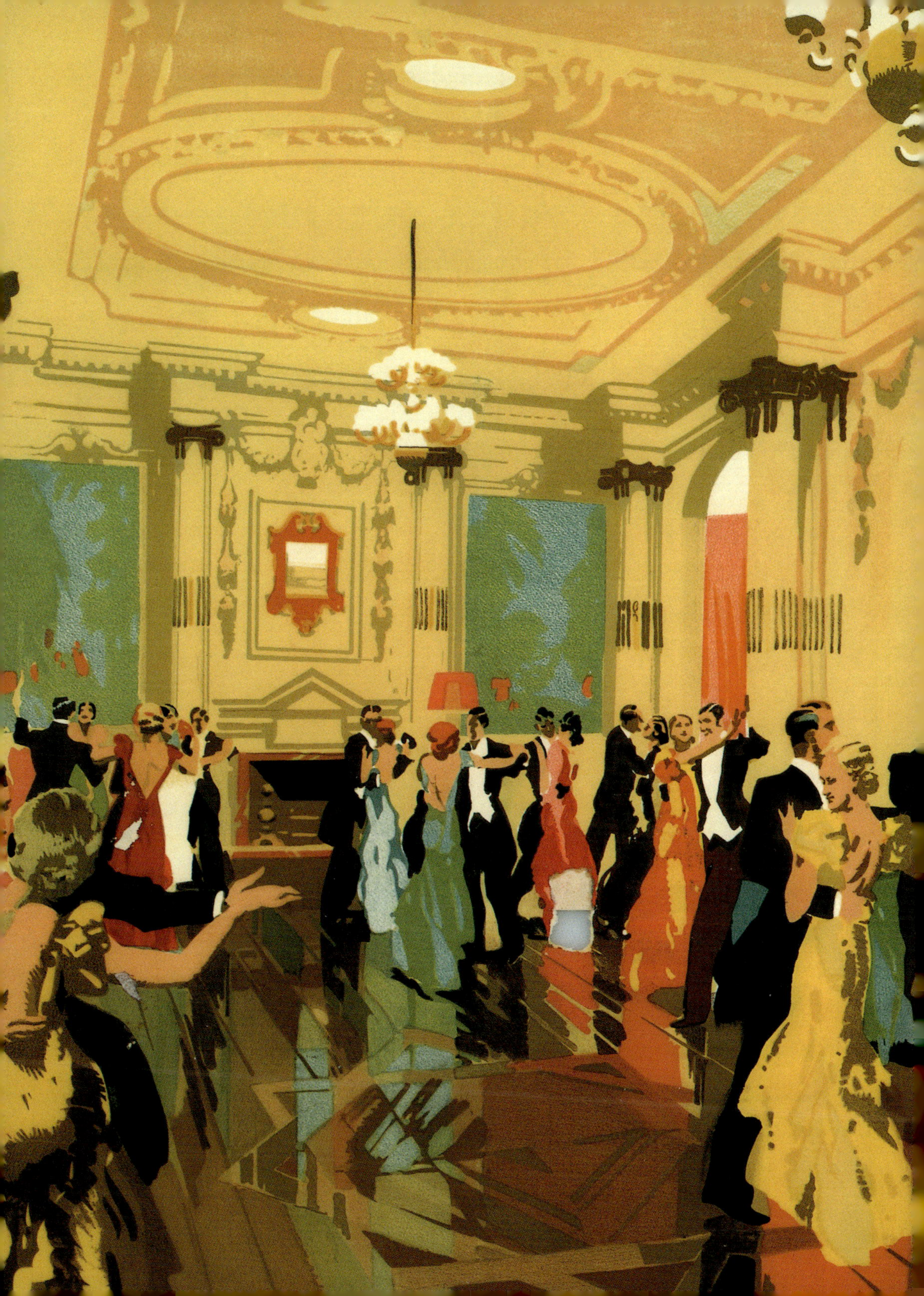

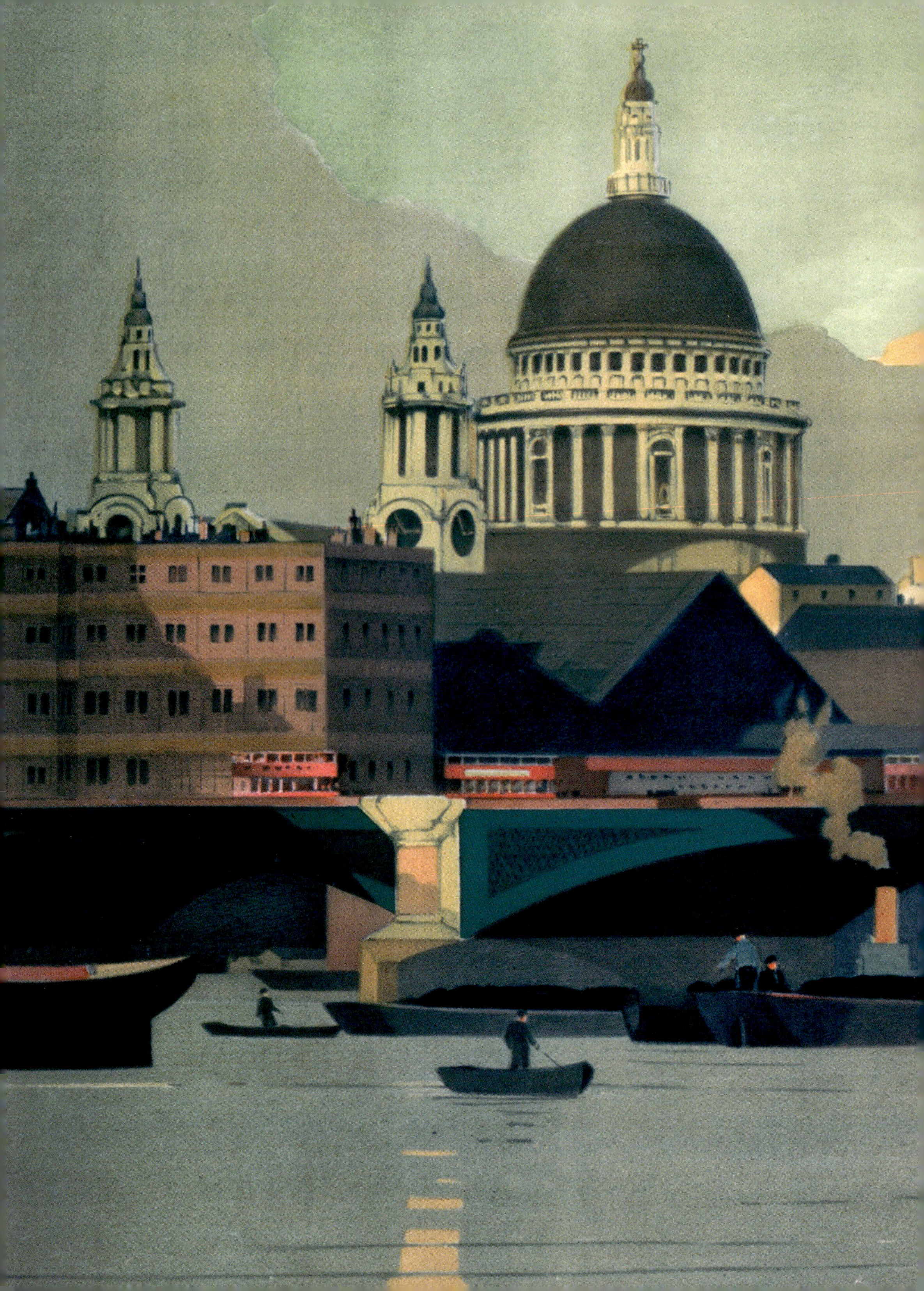

JANUARY

WEEK 1

MONDAY 2
Holiday, UK, Republic of Ireland, Canada, USA, Australia and New Zealand

TUESDAY 3
Holiday, Scotland and New Zealand

WEDNESDAY 4

THURSDAY 5

FRIDAY 6
Epiphany
FIRST QUARTER

SATURDAY 7

SUNDAY 8

A poster by Norman Wilkinson produced by the LMS c.1925 to promote rail services to London. Wilkinson designed posters for several rail companies and organized the Royal Academy series of posters for the LMR in 1924; he was also a famous marine painter.

WEEK 2

JANUARY

9 MONDAY

10 TUESDAY

11 WEDNESDAY

12 THURSDAY

13 FRIDAY

14 SATURDAY
FULL MOON

15 SUNDAY

A 1928 poster by N. Cramer Roberts produced by the Romney, Hythe and Dymchurch Railway, which was founded in Kent in 1927 as a mainline railway in miniature.

DUNGENESS

BY THE ROMNEY, HYTHE AND DYMCHURCH RAILWAY
THE WORLDS SMALLEST PUBLIC RAILWAY

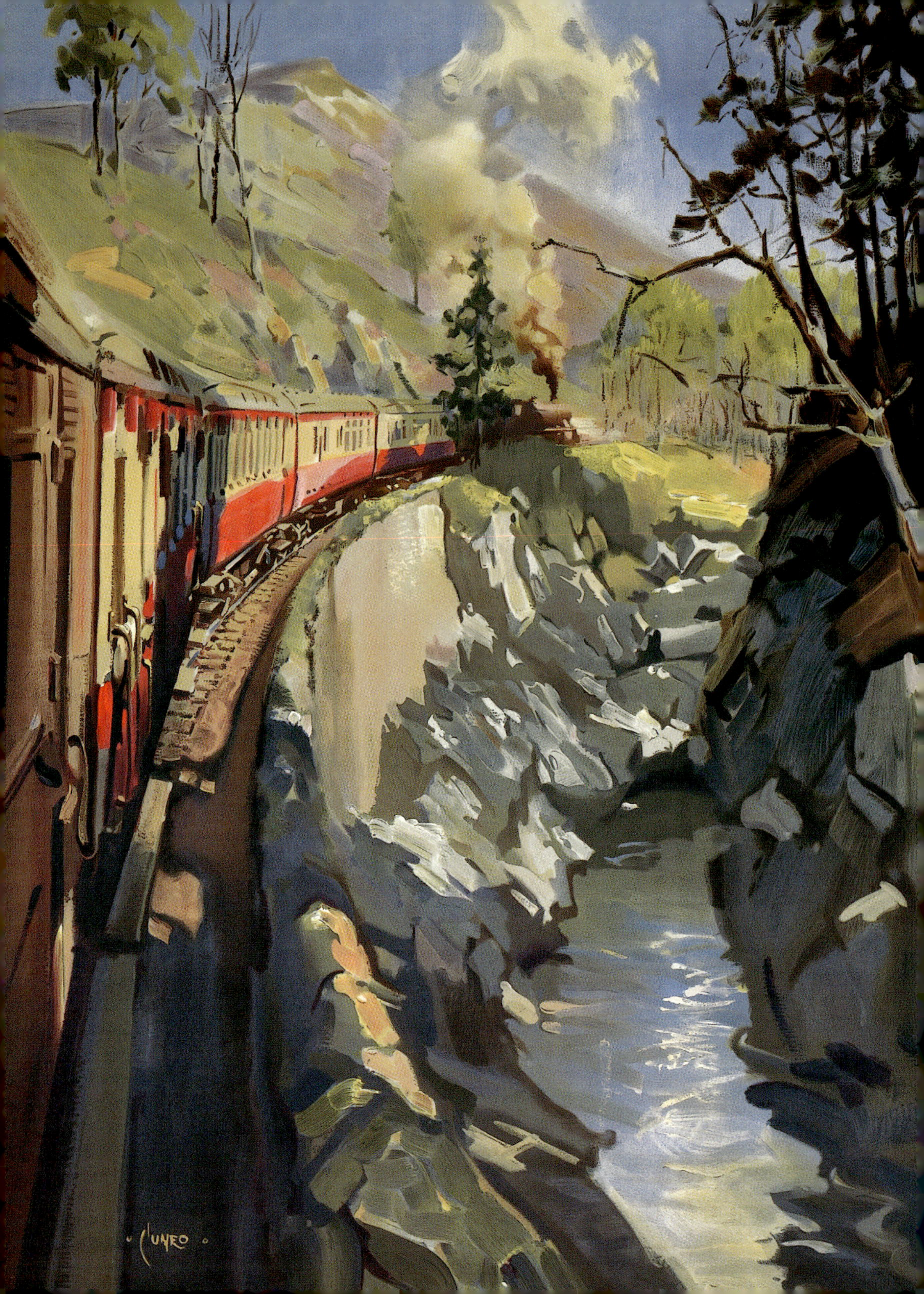
CUNEO

JANUARY

WEEK 3

MONDAY **16**
Holiday, USA (Martin Luther King's birthday)

TUESDAY **17**

WEDNESDAY **18**

THURSDAY **19**

FRIDAY **20**

SATURDAY **21**

SUNDAY **22**
LAST QUARTER

BR produced this poster in the 1950s with the slogan 'By rail to the Highlands'. The artist, Terence Cuneo, was commissioned from the 1940s onwards to paint many railway scenes for posters. He was a prolific painter whose other works include portraits and ceremonial and military subjects.

WEEK 4

JANUARY

23 MONDAY

24 TUESDAY

25 WEDNESDAY

26 THURSDAY
Holiday, Australia (Australia Day)

27 FRIDAY

28 SATURDAY

29 SUNDAY
Chinese New Year
NEW MOON

A poster by Tom Gilfillan produced for the LMS and MacBrayne's Steamers to advertise cruises on the Caledonian Canal in the Scottish Highlands.

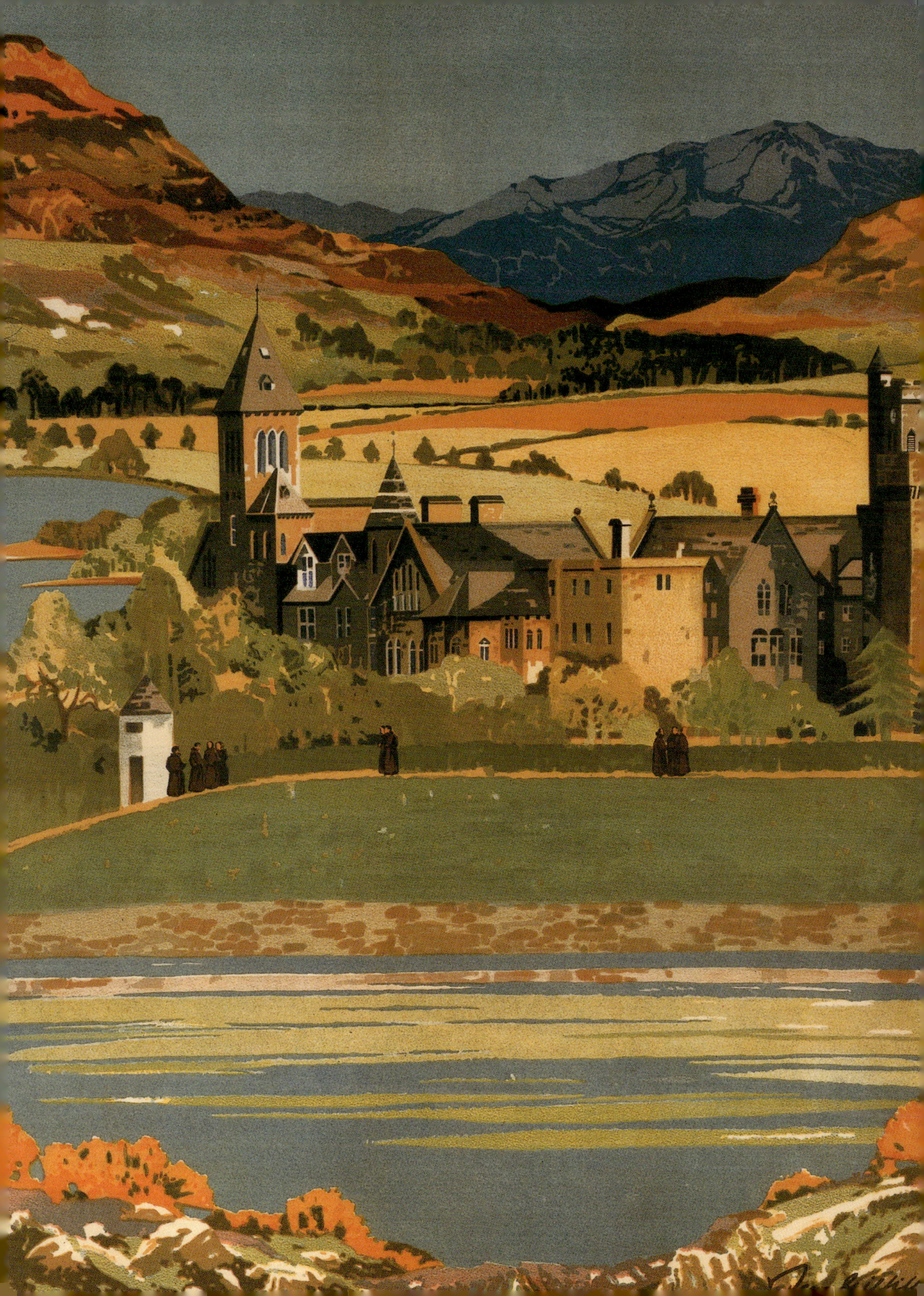

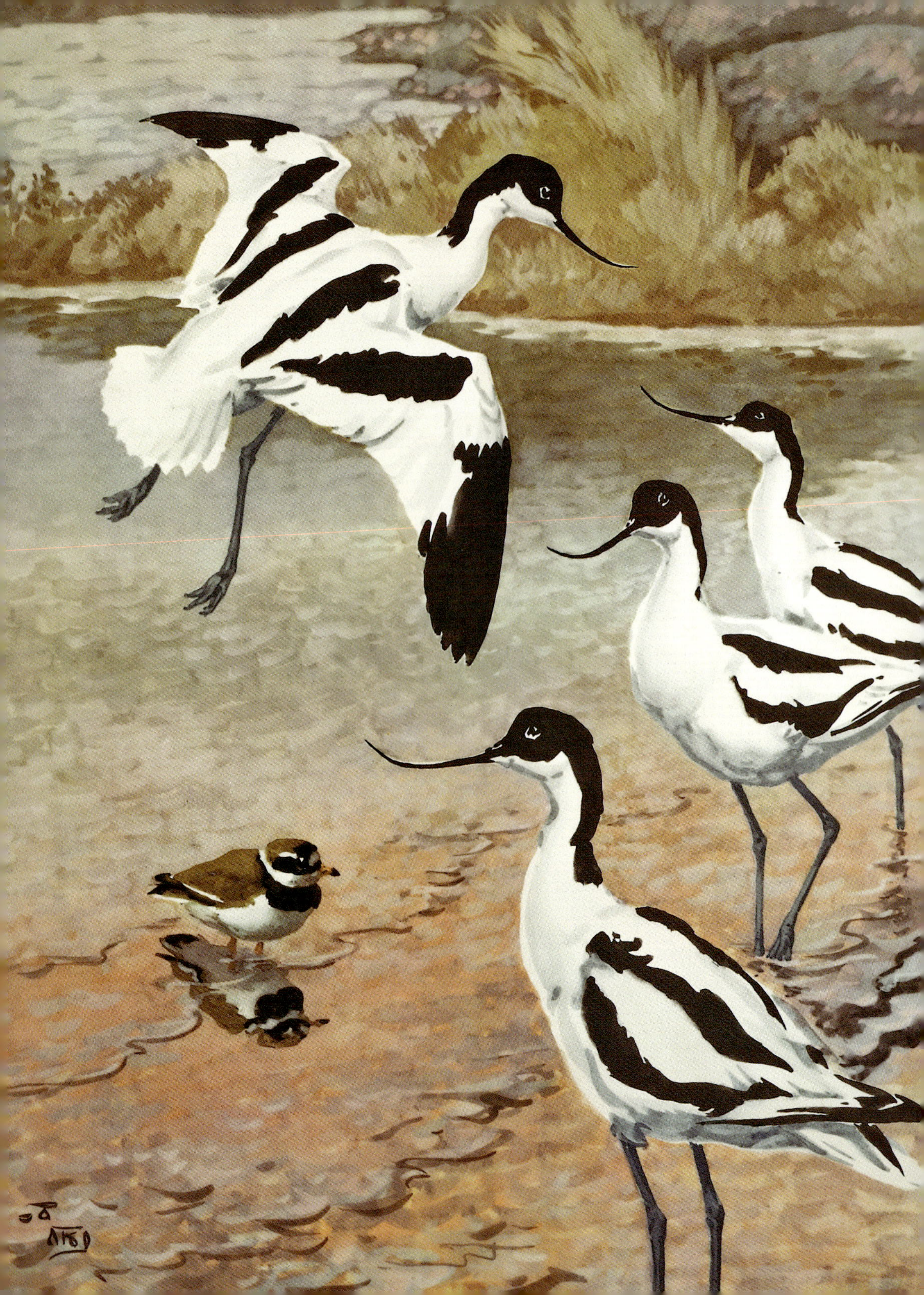

JANUARY & FEBRUARY

WEEK 5

MONDAY **30**

TUESDAY **31**
Islamic New Year (subject to sighting of the moon)

WEDNESDAY **1**

THURSDAY **2**

FRIDAY **3**

SATURDAY **4**

SUNDAY **5**
FIRST QUARTER

A BR poster of the 1950s by Talbot Kelly promoting rail travel to Havergate Island in Suffolk.

WEEK 6

FEBRUARY

6 MONDAY
Holiday, New Zealand (Waitangi Day)

7 TUESDAY

8 WEDNESDAY

9 THURSDAY

10 FRIDAY

11 SATURDAY

12 SUNDAY
Lincoln's birthday

An LNER poster of 1928 by Henry George Gawthorn showing the Forth Bridge, produced to promote rail services to Scotland. As well as illustrating LNER posters Gawthorn wrote several books on poster design. He often included a self-portrait in his posters, complete with pince-nez and a panama hat.

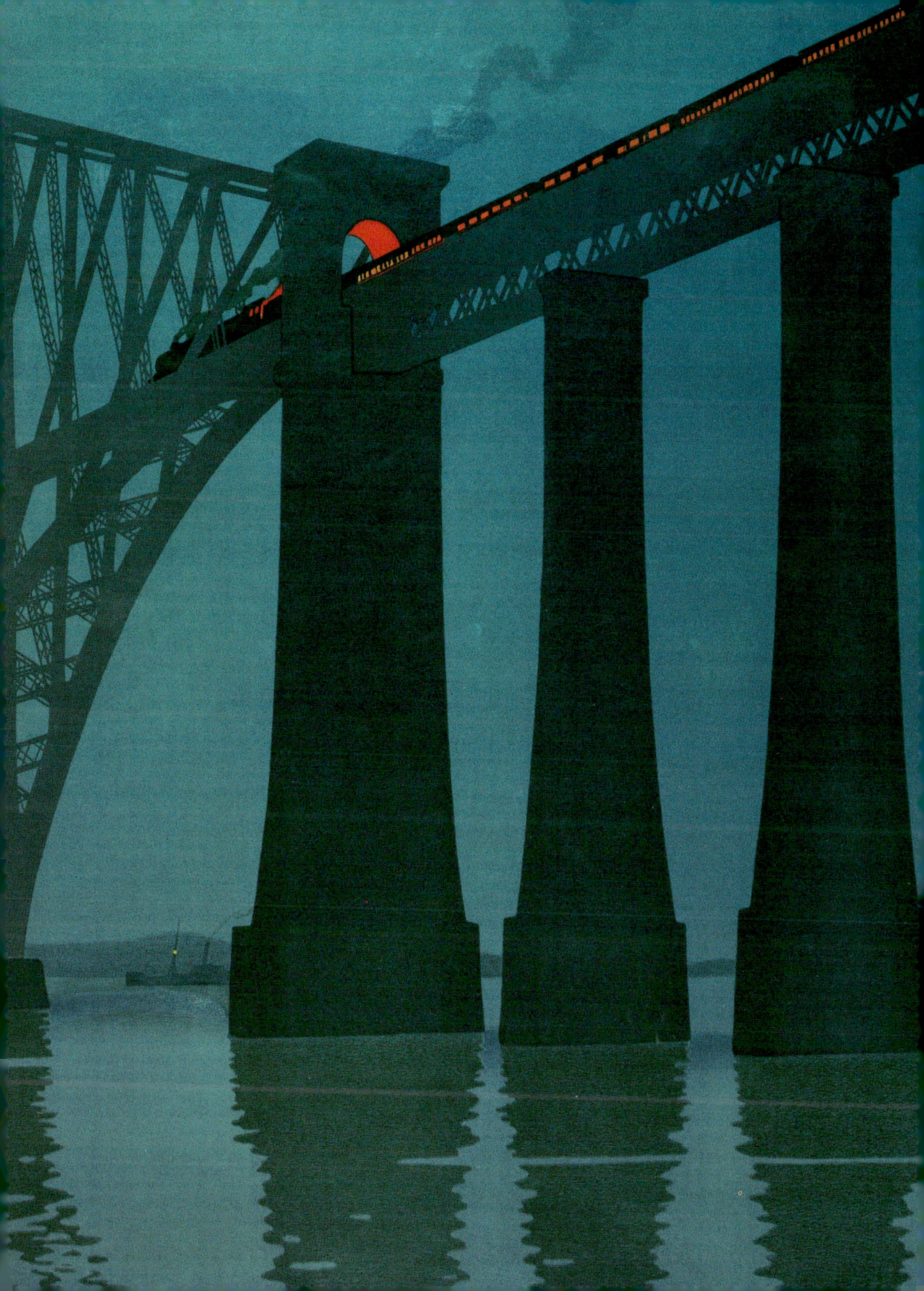

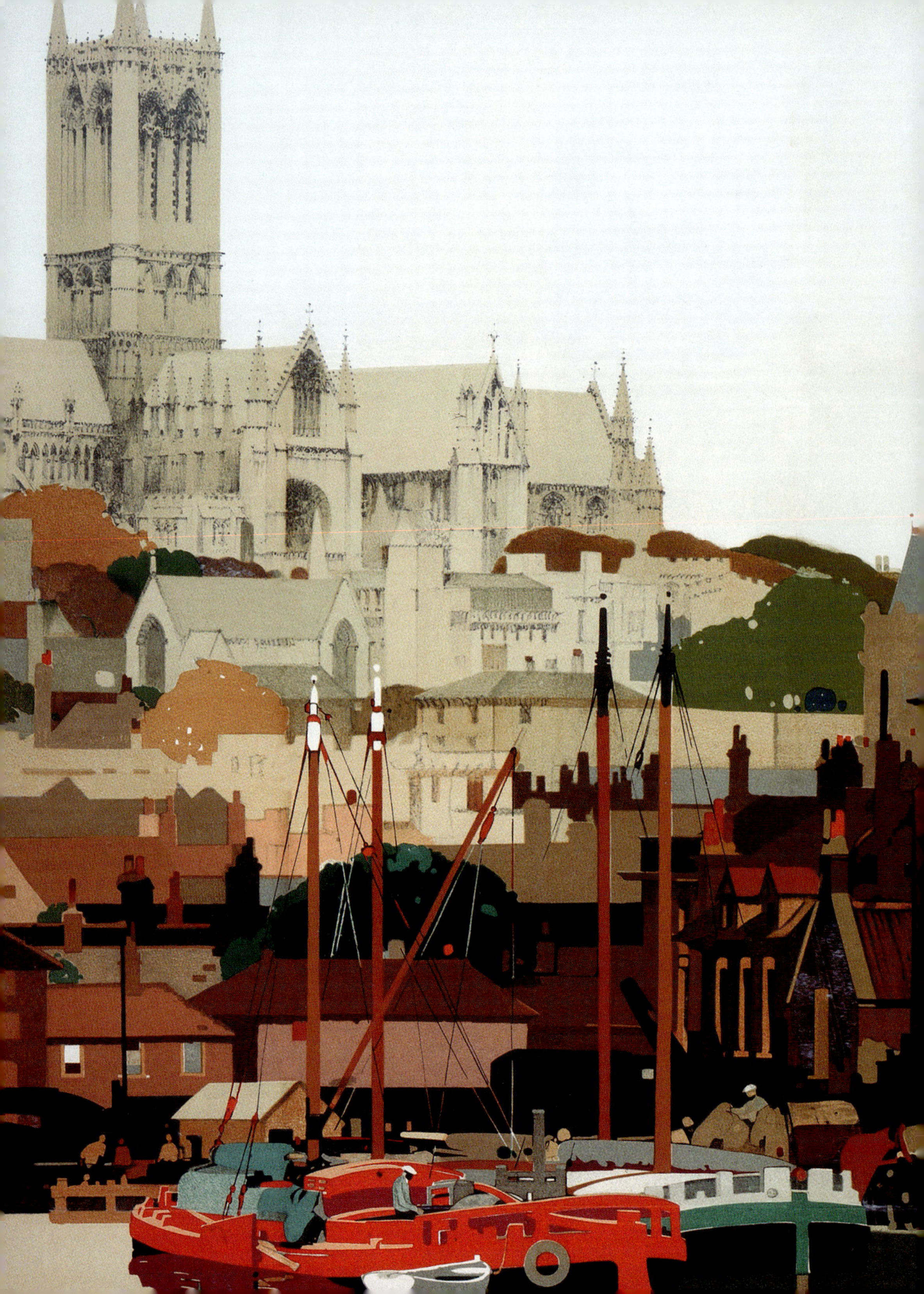

FEBRUARY

WEEK 7

MONDAY 13
Holiday, USA (observed)
FULL MOON

TUESDAY 14
St Valentine's Day

WEDNESDAY 15

THURSDAY 16

FRIDAY 17

SATURDAY 18

SUNDAY 19

'Lincoln by LNER – it's quicker by rail': a poster by Fred Taylor produced in 1924. Taylor also designed ceiling paintings for the Underwriting Room at Lloyd's, exhibited at London galleries and worked for the Empire Marketing Board, London Transport and several shipping companies.

WEEK 8

FEBRUARY

20 MONDAY
Holiday, USA (Presidents' Day)

21 TUESDAY
LAST QUARTER

22 WEDNESDAY

23 THURSDAY

24 FRIDAY

25 SATURDAY

26 SUNDAY

The Tide Mill, Woodbridge, Suffolk by Jack Merriott, a BR poster of the 1950s promoting rail travel to Suffolk.

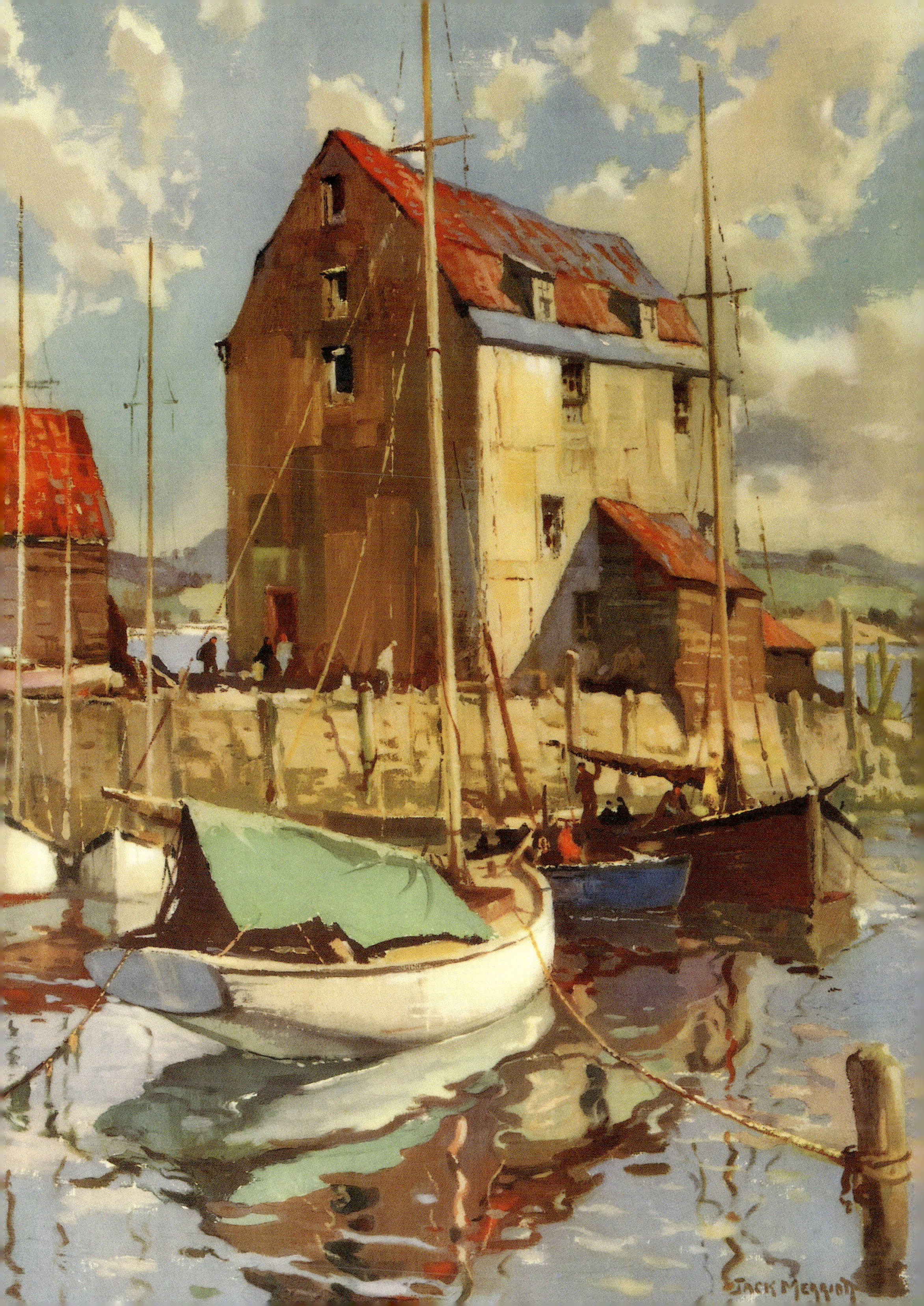
JACK MERRIOTT

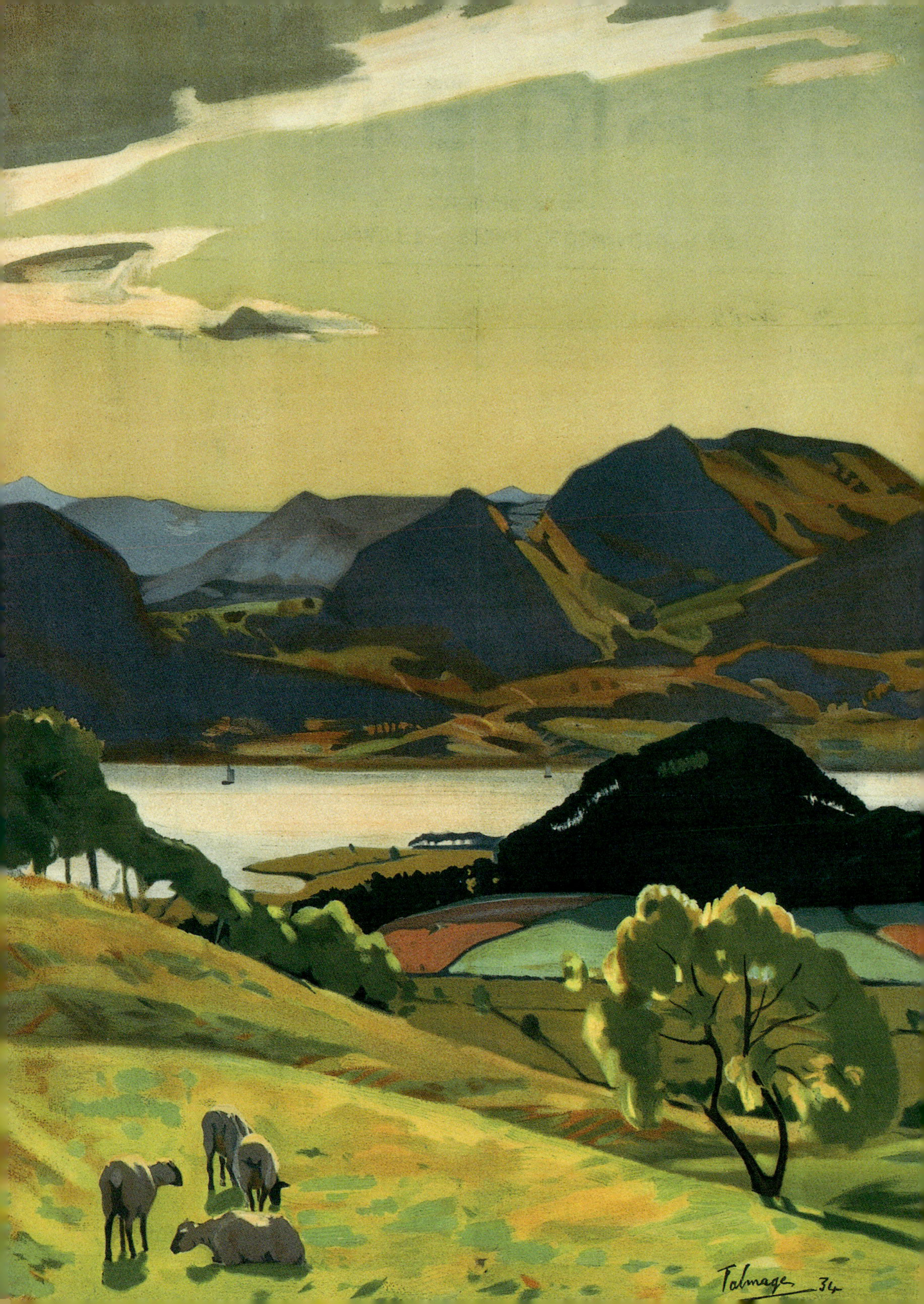
Talmage 34

FEBRUARY & MARCH

WEEK 9

MONDAY **27**

TUESDAY **28**
Shrove Tuesday
NEW MOON

WEDNESDAY **1**
Ash Wednesday
St David's Day

THURSDAY **2**

FRIDAY **3**

SATURDAY **4**

SUNDAY **5**

An LMS poster by Algernon Mayow Talmage which appeared with the slogan 'The Lake District for holidays – Derwentwater from Keswick Hill'.

WEEK 10

MARCH

6 MONDAY
FIRST QUARTER

7 TUESDAY

8 WEDNESDAY

9 THURSDAY

10 FRIDAY

11 SATURDAY

12 SUNDAY

Promoting Whitley Bay, this poster was produced in 1933 by the LNER. As well as designing railway posters the artist, Frank Henry Mason, painted marine and coastal subjects and was involved in engineering and shipbuilding in Leeds and Hartlepool.

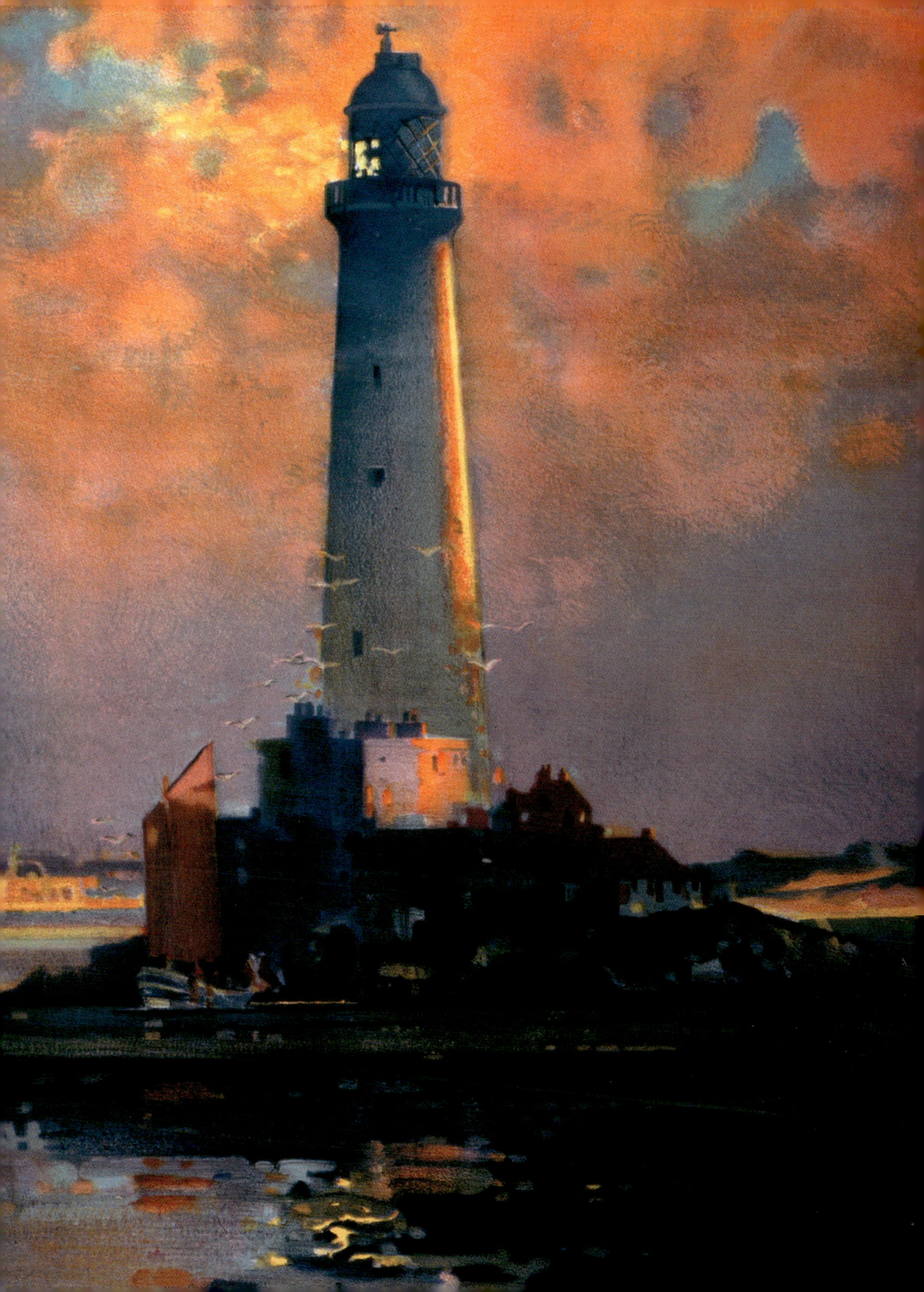

OBSERVATION CAR

MARCH

WEEK 11

MONDAY 13
Commonwealth Day

TUESDAY 14
FULL MOON

WEDNESDAY 15

THURSDAY 16

FRIDAY 17
St Patrick's Day
Holiday, Northern Ireland and Republic of Ireland

SATURDAY 18

SUNDAY 19

BR's poster by Jack Merriott promoted the West Highland Line in 1959. It shows a train of observation coaches crossing the Lochy Viaduct near Fort William.

WEEK 12

MARCH

20 MONDAY
Vernal Equinox

21 TUESDAY

22 WEDNESDAY
LAST QUARTER

23 THURSDAY

24 FRIDAY

25 SATURDAY

26 SUNDAY
Mothering Sunday, UK
British Summertime begins

A poster by Adrian Allinson jointly produced in 1936 by the GWR and the SR to promote rail travel to Cornwall.

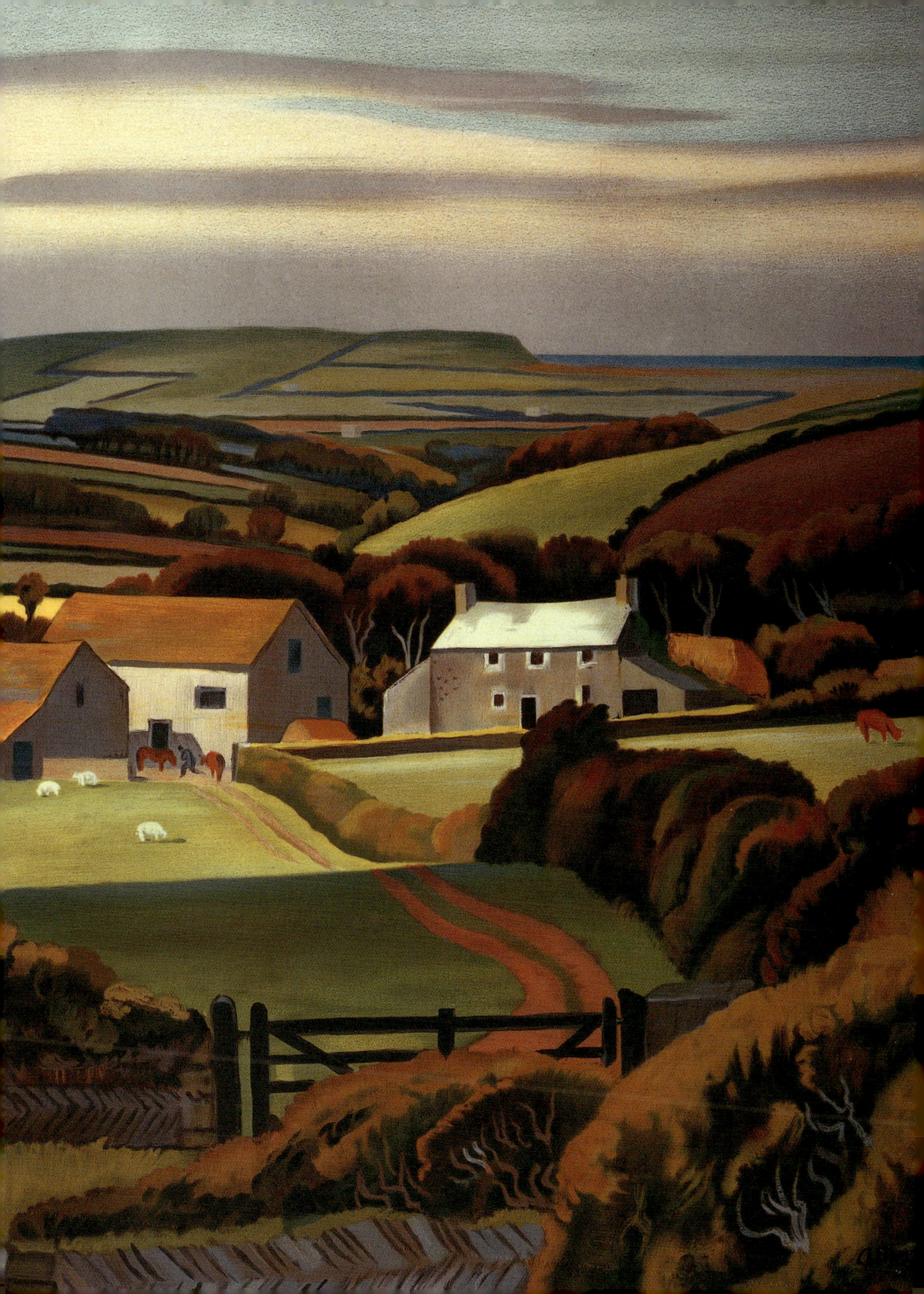

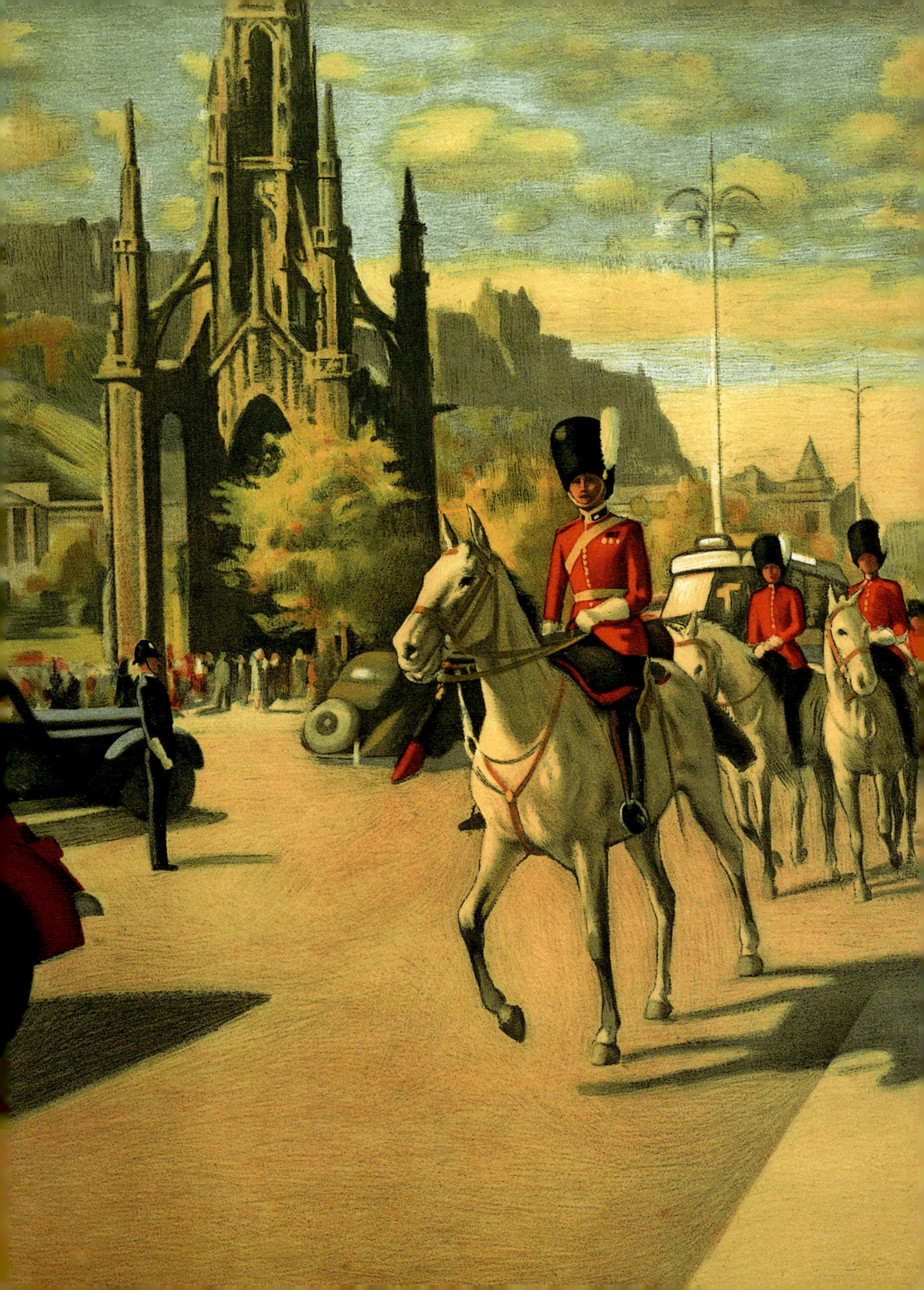

MARCH & APRIL

WEEK 13

MONDAY **27**

TUESDAY **28**

WEDNESDAY **29**
NEW MOON

THURSDAY **30**

FRIDAY **31**

SATURDAY **1**

SUNDAY **2**

An LNER poster of Edinburgh by Michael, 1934.

WEEK 14

APRIL

3 MONDAY

4 TUESDAY

5 WEDNESDAY
FIRST QUARTER

6 THURSDAY

7 FRIDAY

8 SATURDAY

9 SUNDAY
Palm Sunday

Norman Wilkinson's painting of Lake Windermere promoted travel to the Lake District on the LMS. The poster also advertised services operated by LMS steamers travelling from Lake Side to Bowness and to Waterhead Pier, Ambleside.

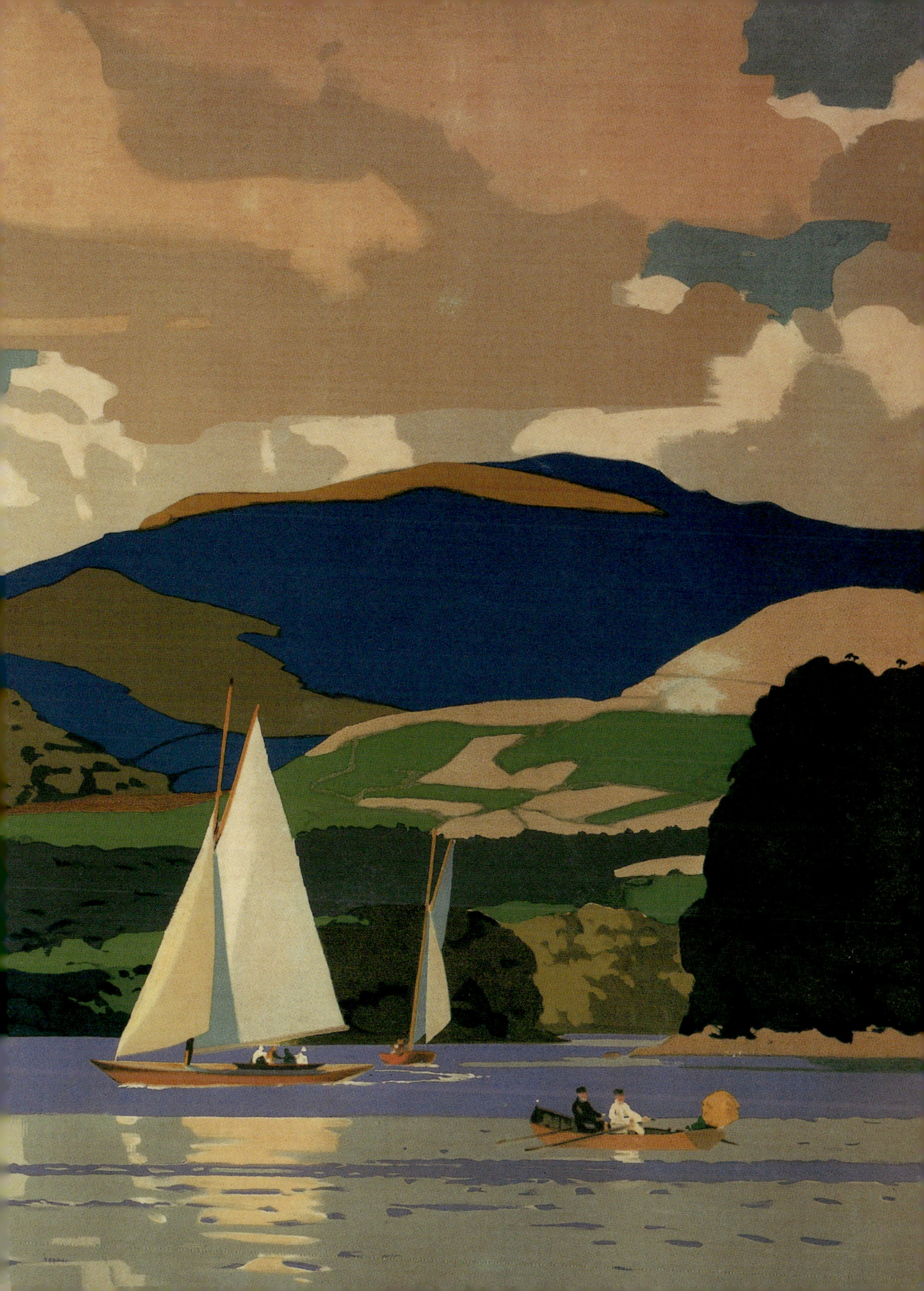

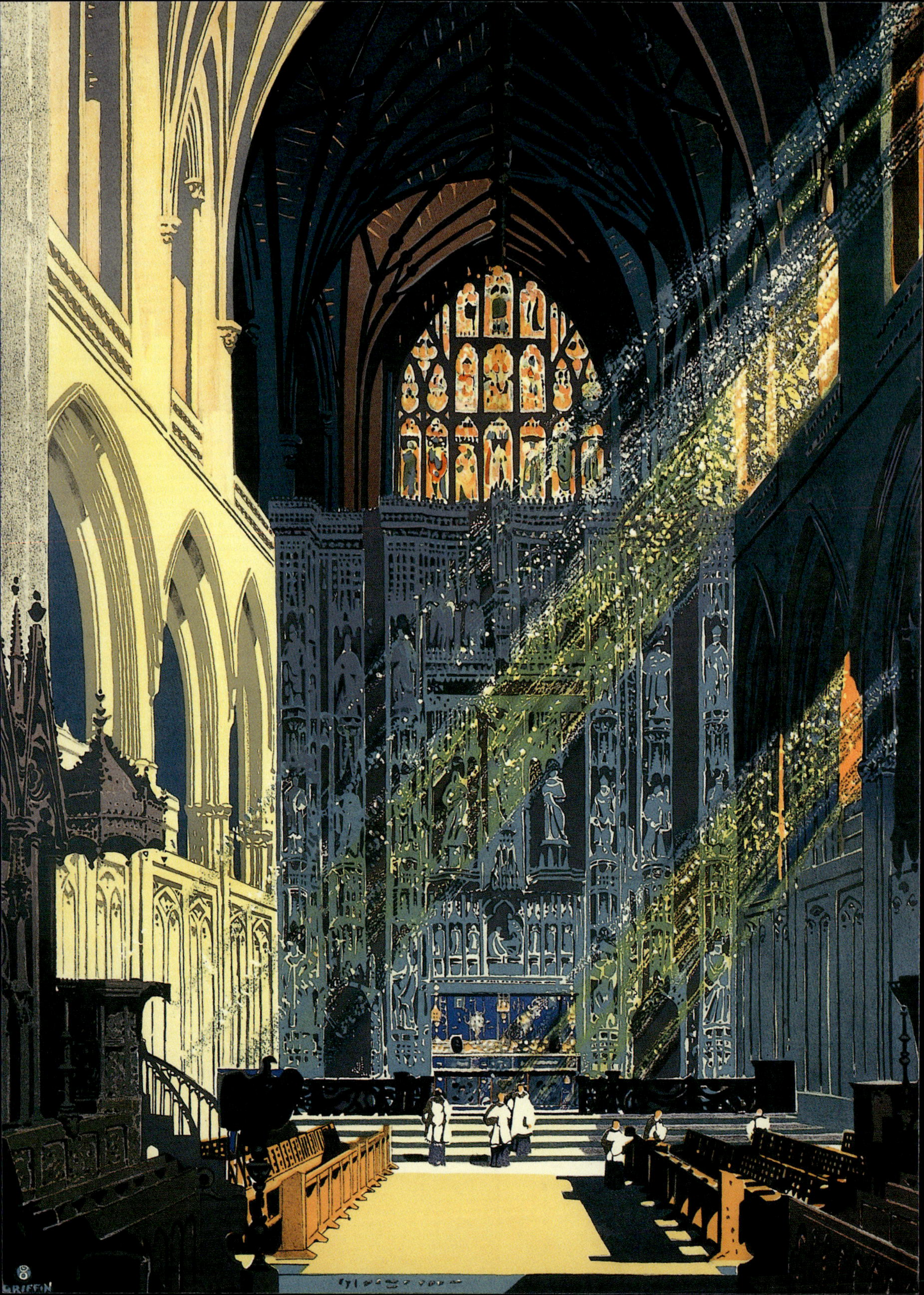
GRIFFIN

APRIL

WEEK 15

MONDAY 10

TUESDAY 11

WEDNESDAY 12

THURSDAY 13
Maundy Thursday
Passover (Pesach), First Day
FULL MOON

FRIDAY 14
Good Friday
Holiday, UK, Republic of Ireland,
Canada, USA, Australia and New Zealand

SATURDAY 15

SUNDAY 16
Easter Sunday

An SR poster of Winchester Cathedral by Griffin, 1935.

WEEK 16

APRIL

17 MONDAY
Easter Monday
Holiday, UK (exc. Scotland), Republic of Ireland,
Canada, Australia and New Zealand

18 TUESDAY

19 WEDNESDAY
Passover (Pesach), Seventh Day

20 THURSDAY
Passover (Pesach), Eighth Day

21 FRIDAY
Birthday of Queen Elizabeth II
LAST QUARTER

22 SATURDAY

23 SUNDAY
St George's Day

An LMS poster of the 1920s by Harry Hudson Rodmell.

TO JOIN
THESE CRUISES
TRAVEL LMS
THE WESTERN
HIGHLANDS
OF SCOTLAND
BY
KINLOCHBERVIE
BADCALL
LEWIS
STORNOWAY
LOCHINVER
BADEN TARBET
ULLAPOOL
HARRIS
TARBERT
RODEL
AULTBEA
GAIRLOCH
N.UIST
LOCHMADDY
STAFFIN
BENBECULA
DUNVEGAN
SKYE
PORTREE
APPLECROSS
INVERNESS
KYLE OF LOCHALSH
TEMPLE PIER
GLEN URQUHART
BROADFORD
GLENELG
FOYERS
LOCHBOISDALE
LOCH CORUISK
CANNA
ARMADALE
LOCH SCAVAIG
RUM
CALEDONIAN CANAL
(WONDER WATERWAY)
LOCH NESS
FORT AUGUSTUS
KISMUL CASTLE
CASTLEBAY
MALLAIG
LOCH LOCHY
EIGG
BANAVIE
MUCK
FORT WILLIAM
KINLOCHLEVEN
GLENCOE
COLL
KILCHOAN
TOBERMORY
KENTALLEN
APPIN
TIREE
SALEN
STAFFA
MULL
OBAN
TYNDRUM
IONA
CRIANLARICH
ARDLUI
INVERARAY
TARBET
JURA
BALLOCH
CRAIGENDORAN
DUNOON
PORT ASKAIG
KYLES OF BUTE
GREENOCK
GOUROCK
TARBERT
ROTHESAY
GLASGOW
EDINBURGH
ISLAY
PORT ELLEN
ARRAN
ROYAL MAIL SERVICES
MACBRAYNES
HARRY HUDSON RODMELL
THE ROYAL ROUTE
STEAMERS
ALL PARTICULARS FROM
DAVID MACBRAYNE LTD
CLYDE HOUSE · GLASGOW

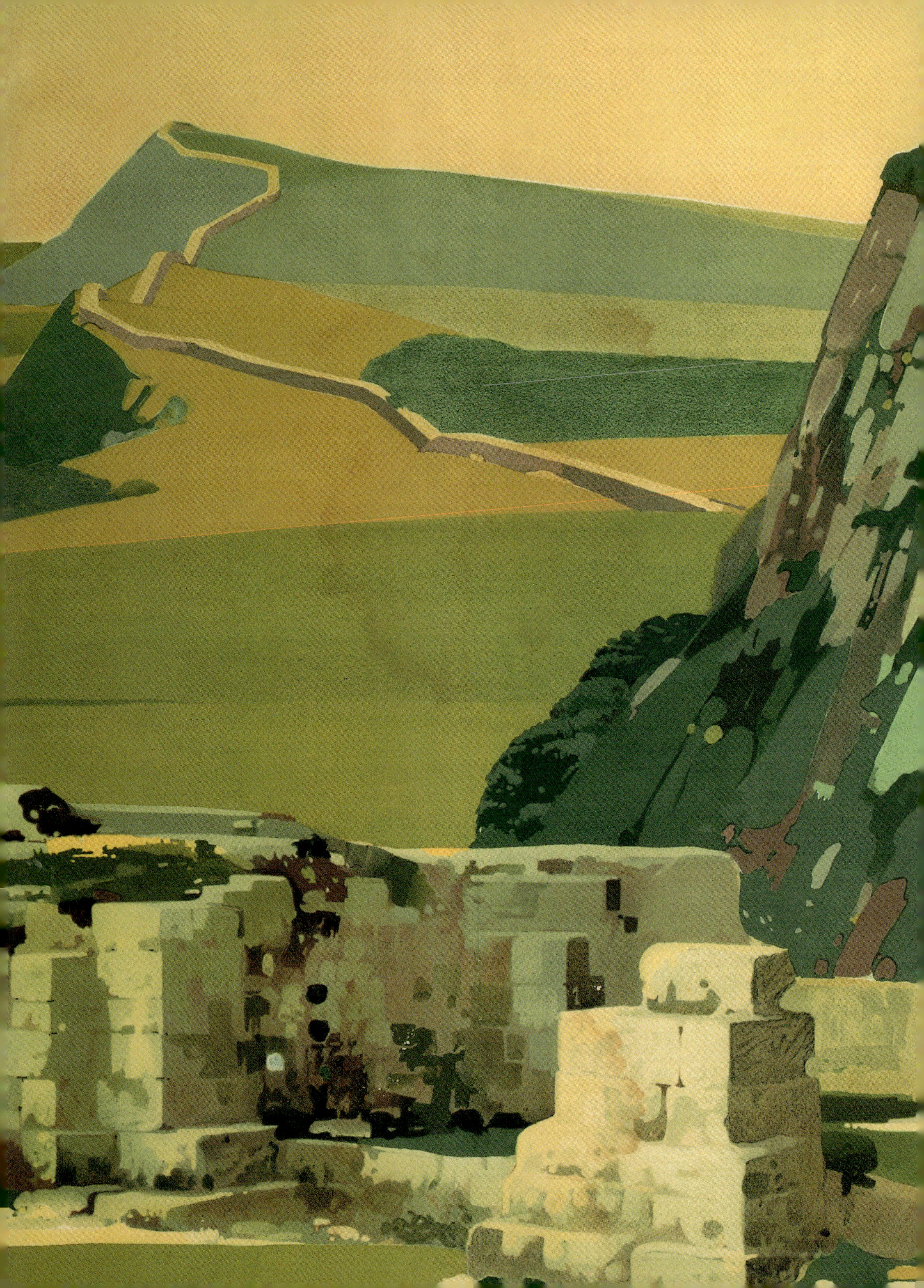

APRIL

WEEK 17

MONDAY **24**

TUESDAY **25**
Holiday, Australia and New Zealand (Anzac Day)

WEDNESDAY **26**

THURSDAY **27**
NEW MOON

FRIDAY **28**

SATURDAY **29**

SUNDAY **30**

The Road of the Roman, by Fred Taylor, 1930, produced by the LNER to promote train services to Newcastle.

WEEK 18

MAY

1 MONDAY
Early May Bank Holiday, UK and Republic of Ireland

2 TUESDAY

3 WEDNESDAY

4 THURSDAY

5 FRIDAY
FIRST QUARTER

6 SATURDAY

7 SUNDAY

A view of the bridge over the River Eden, Carlisle. The LMS and LNER jointly produced this poster by an unknown artist to promote rail travel to the city.

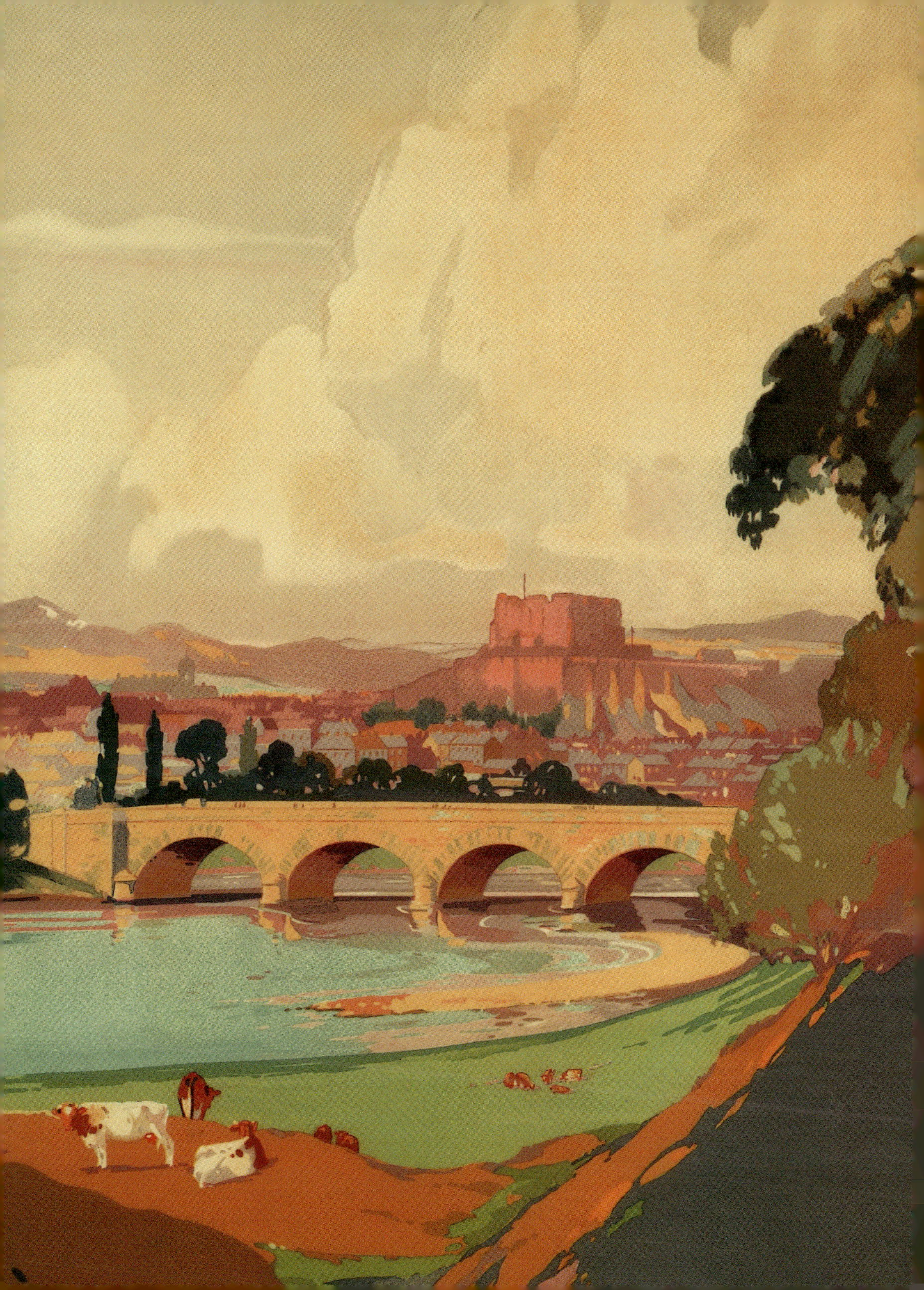

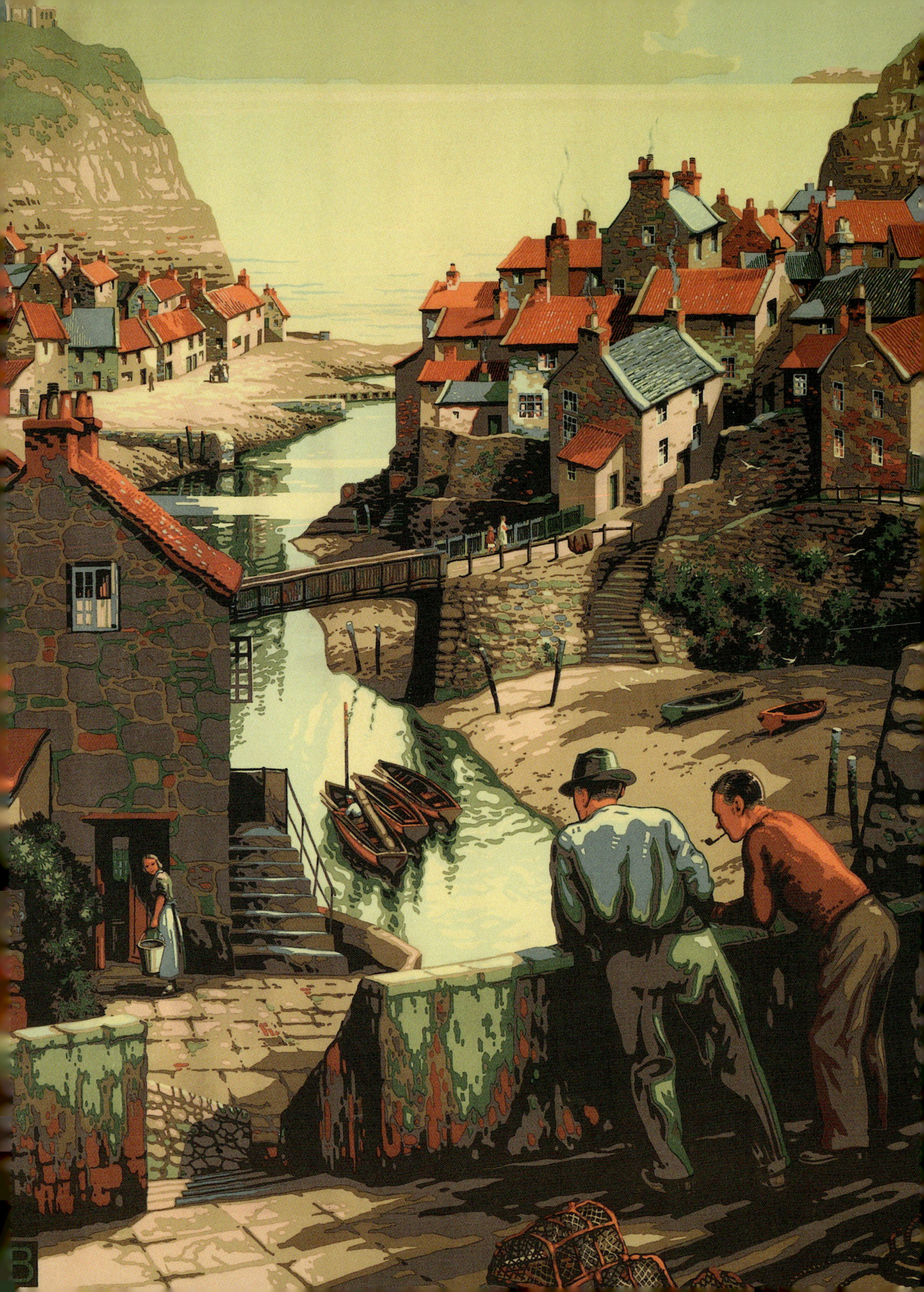

MAY

WEEK 19

MONDAY 8

TUESDAY 9

WEDNESDAY 10

THURSDAY 11

FRIDAY 12

SATURDAY 13
FULL MOON

SUNDAY 14
Mother's Day, Canada, USA, Australia and New Zealand

A BR poster by John Bee promoting rail services to the Yorkshire coast.

WEEK 20

MAY

15 MONDAY

16 TUESDAY

17 WEDNESDAY

18 THURSDAY

19 FRIDAY

20 SATURDAY
LAST QUARTER

21 SUNDAY

An SR poster, 1923, promoting Dorset and Devon as holiday destinations.

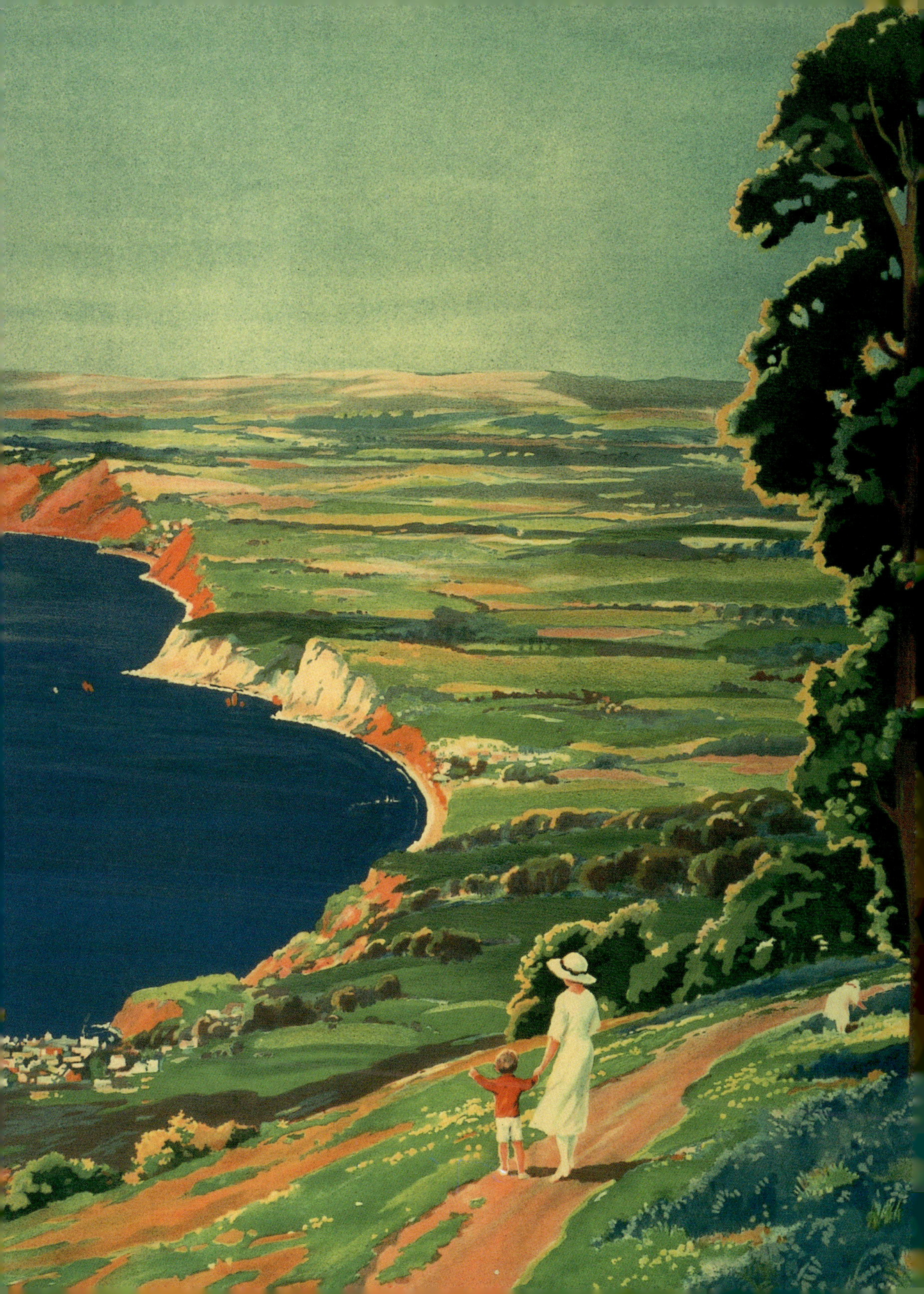

THE LONDONER'S LEISURE – THE THAMES

CHEAP DAY TICKETS TO THE UP-RIVER RESORTS BY SOUTHERN RAILWAY

FROM WATERLOO & SUBURBAN STATIONS

H·A·WALKER GENERAL MANAGER

MAY

WEEK 21

MONDAY 22

TUESDAY 23

WEDNESDAY 24

THURSDAY 25
Ascension Day

FRIDAY 26

SATURDAY 27
NEW MOON

SUNDAY 28

An SR poster of 1926 by F. Gregory Brown, who was a landscape painter, illustrator, metal worker and textile designer.

WEEK 22

MAY & JUNE

29 MONDAY
Spring Bank Holiday, UK
Holiday, USA (Memorial Day)

30 TUESDAY

31 WEDNESDAY

1 THURSDAY

2 FRIDAY
Jewish Feast of Weeks (Shavuot)

3 SATURDAY
FIRST QUARTER

4 SUNDAY
Whit Sunday (Pentecost)

With the slogan ' Edinburgh – it's quicker by rail' this poster promoted LNER and LMS rail services to the city in 1934. The artist, Henry Rushby, was a watercolourist, etcher and drypoint artist who favoured architectural scenes.

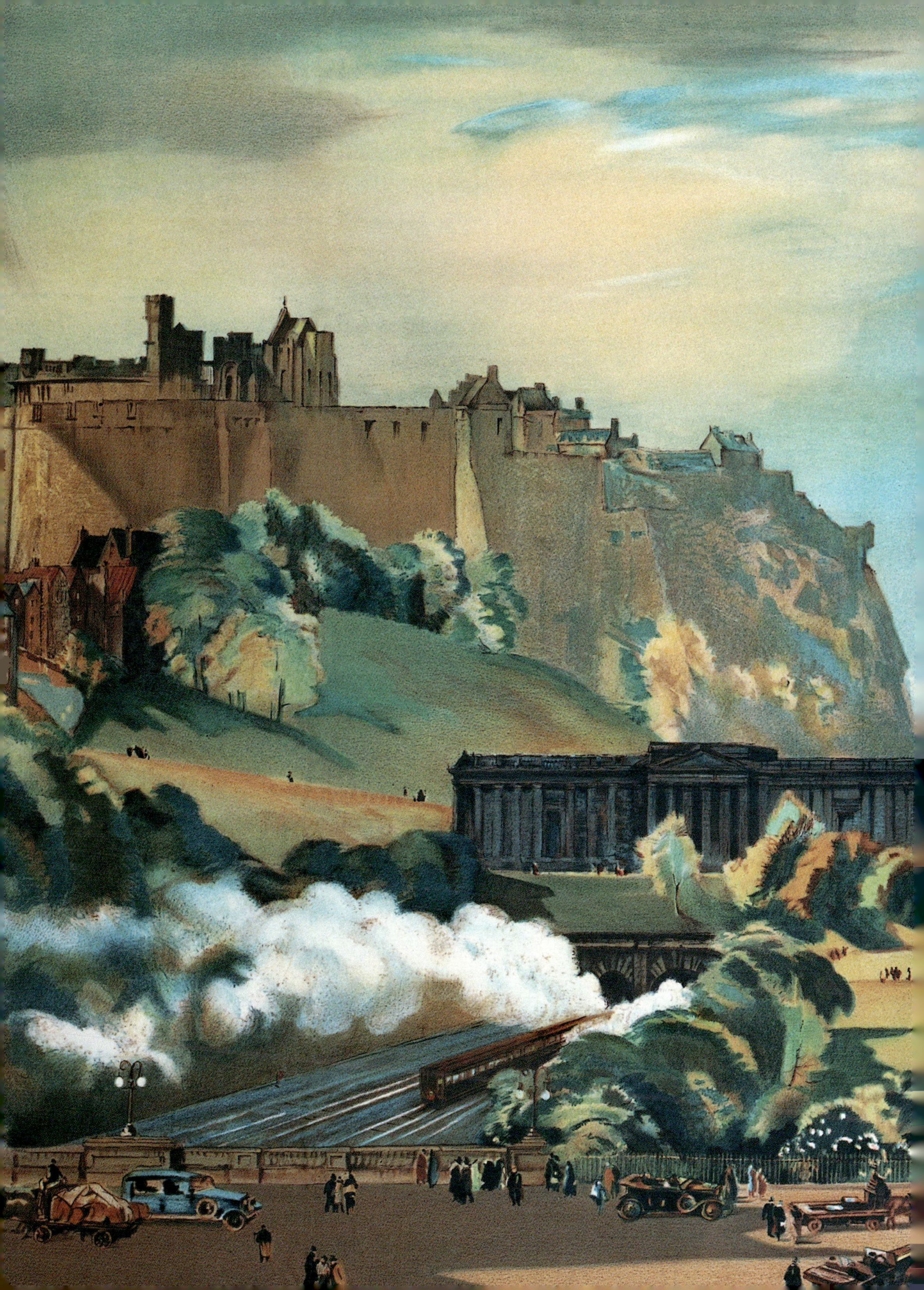

"WEST RIDING LIMITED"

THE FIRST STREAMLINE TRAIN
BRADFORD LEEDS LONDON
[KING'S CROSS]

MONDAYS TO FRIDAYS
commencing 27th September 1937

	a.m.		p.m.
BRADFORD EXCHANGE	dep. 11.10	**LONDON** KING'S CROSS	dep. 7.10
LEEDS CENTRAL	dep. 11.31	**LEEDS** CENTRAL	arr. 9.53
LONDON KING'S CROSS	arr. 2.15 p.m.	**BRADFORD** EXCHANGE	arr. 10.15

LONDON & NORTH EASTERN RAILWAY

JUNE

WEEK 23

MONDAY 5
Holiday, Republic of Ireland
Holiday, New Zealand (The Queen's birthday)

TUESDAY 6

WEDNESDAY 7

THURSDAY 8

FRIDAY 9

SATURDAY 10
The Queen's official birthday (subject to confirmation)

SUNDAY 11
Trinity Sunday
FULL MOON

A poster produced for LNER in 1938. The artist was Charles 'Shep' Shepherd, who also designed posters for the Royal Mail Packet Steam Company, London Transport and SR.

WEEK 24

JUNE

12 MONDAY
Holiday, Australia (The Queen's birthday)

13 TUESDAY

14 WEDNESDAY

15 THURSDAY
Corpus Christi

16 FRIDAY

17 SATURDAY

18 SUNDAY
Father's Day, UK, Canada and USA
LAST QUARTER

Austin Cooper's view of Whitby promoted rail travel to the North Yorkshire town for the LNER. After an early career as a commercial artist, Cooper designed posters for LNER, Indian State Railways and London Transport.

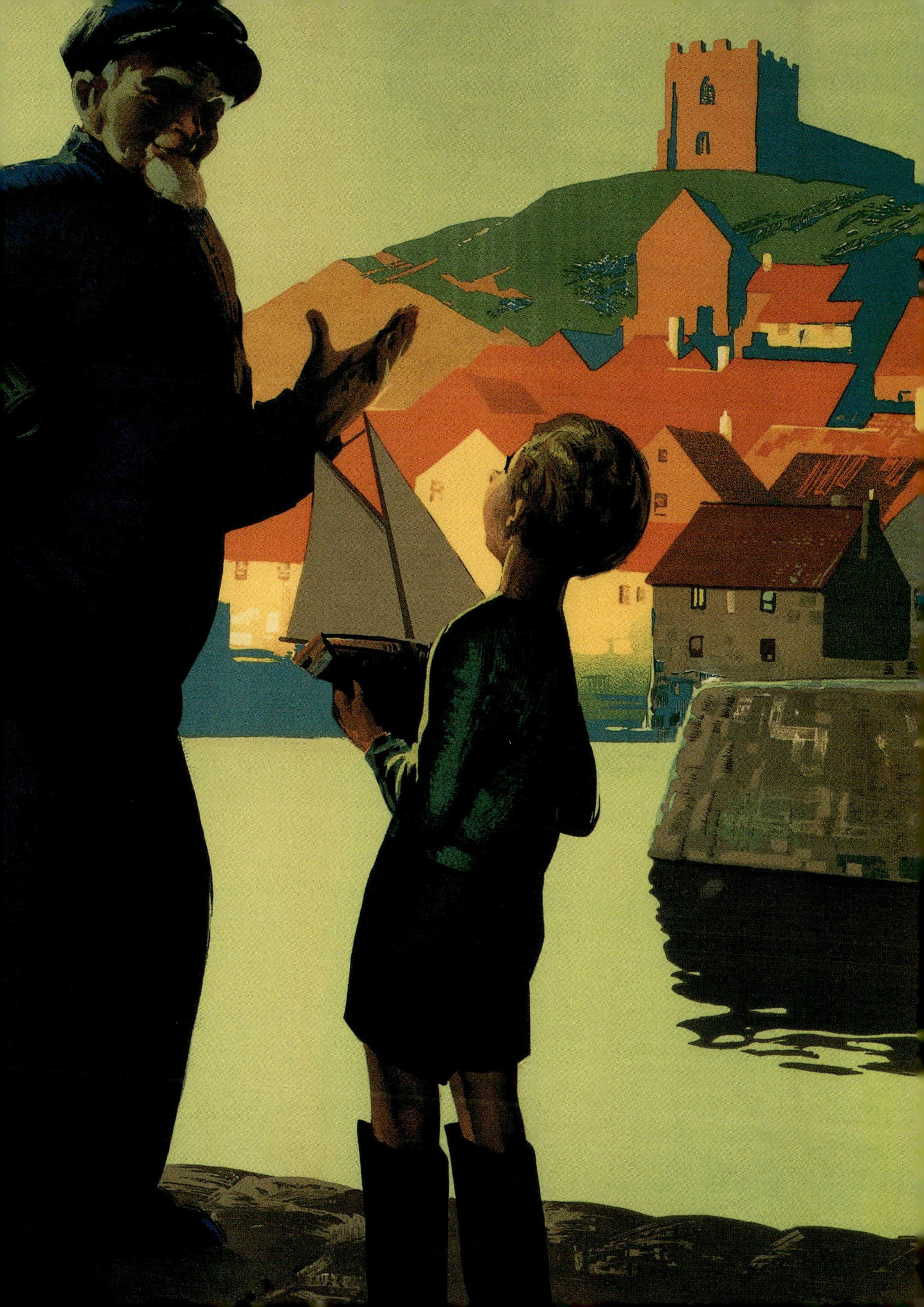

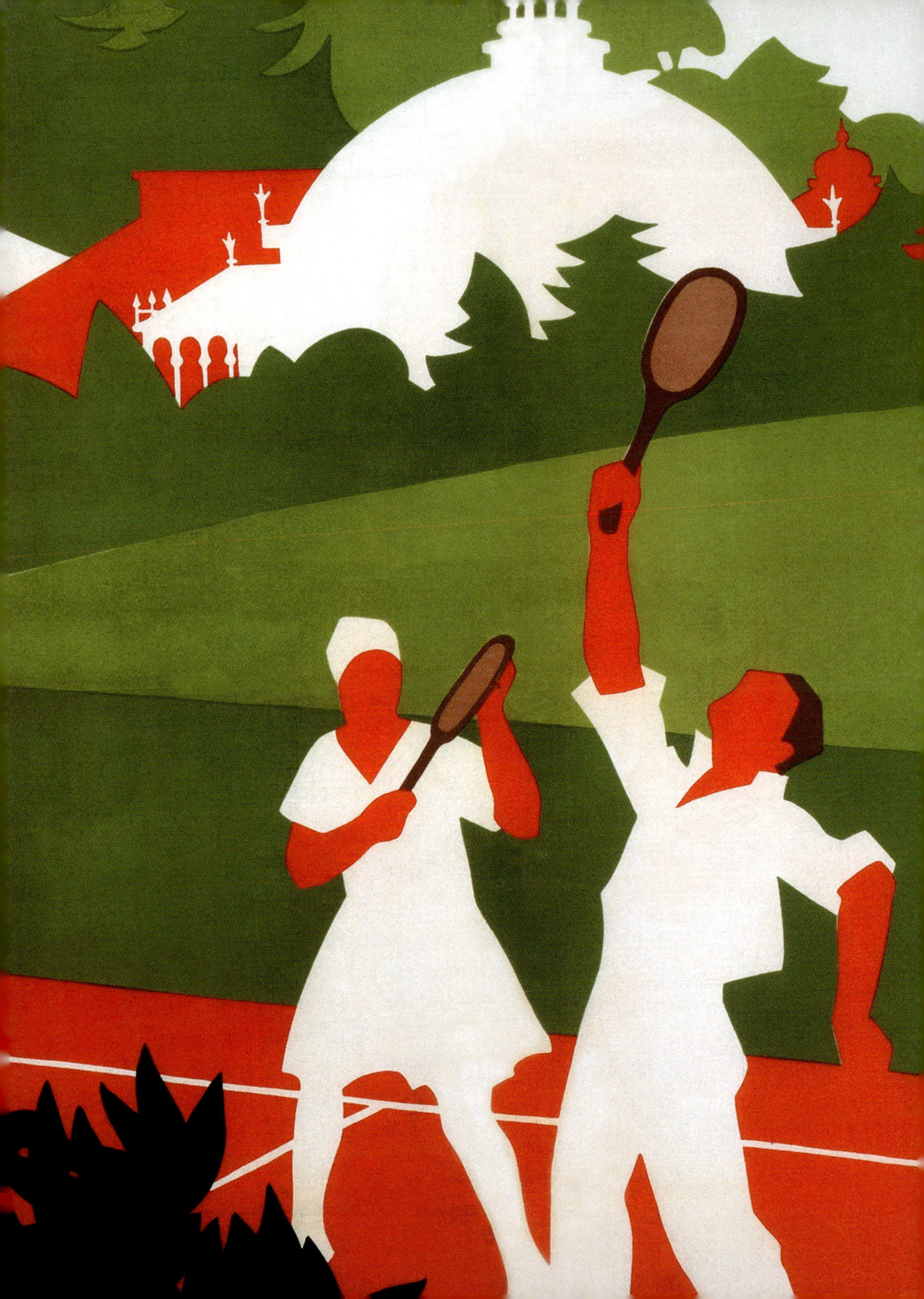

JUNE

WEEK 25

MONDAY **19**

TUESDAY **20**

WEDNESDAY **21**
Summer Solstice

THURSDAY **22**

FRIDAY **23**

SATURDAY **24**

SUNDAY **25**
NEW MOON

An LNER poster, c.1930, advertising rail travel to the Yorkshire spa town of Harrogate. The artist was Tom Purvis, who rallied for the professionalization of commercial art, was one of a group of artists who founded the Society of Industrial Artists (which campaigned for improved standards of training for commercial arts) and became one of the first Royal Designers for Industry.

WEEK 26

JUNE & JULY

26 MONDAY

27 TUESDAY

28 WEDNESDAY

29 THURSDAY

30 FRIDAY

1 SATURDAY
Holiday, Canada (Canada Day)

2 SUNDAY

An LNER poster of 1928 by Fred Taylor promoting rail travel to Bridlington, Yorkshire.

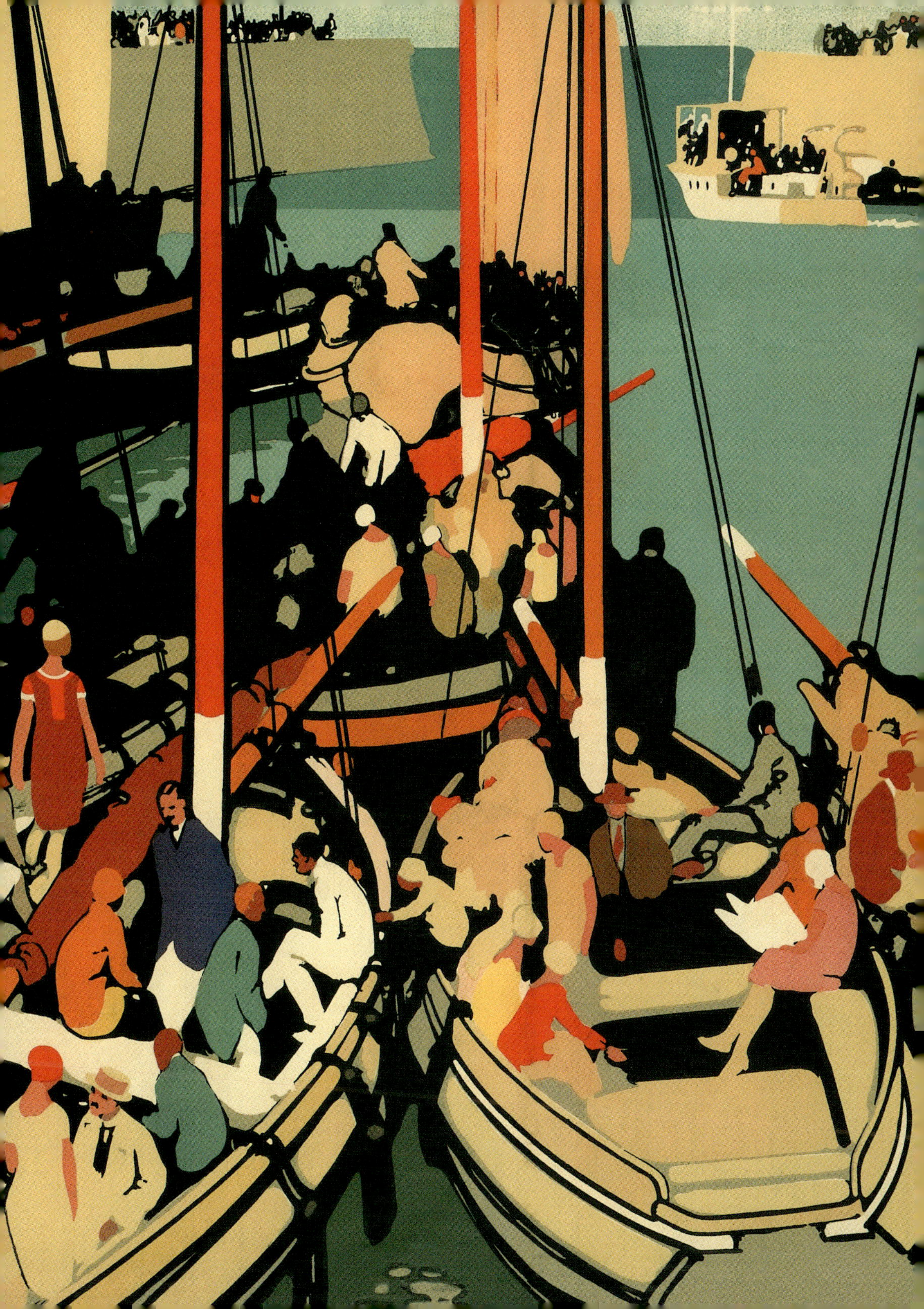

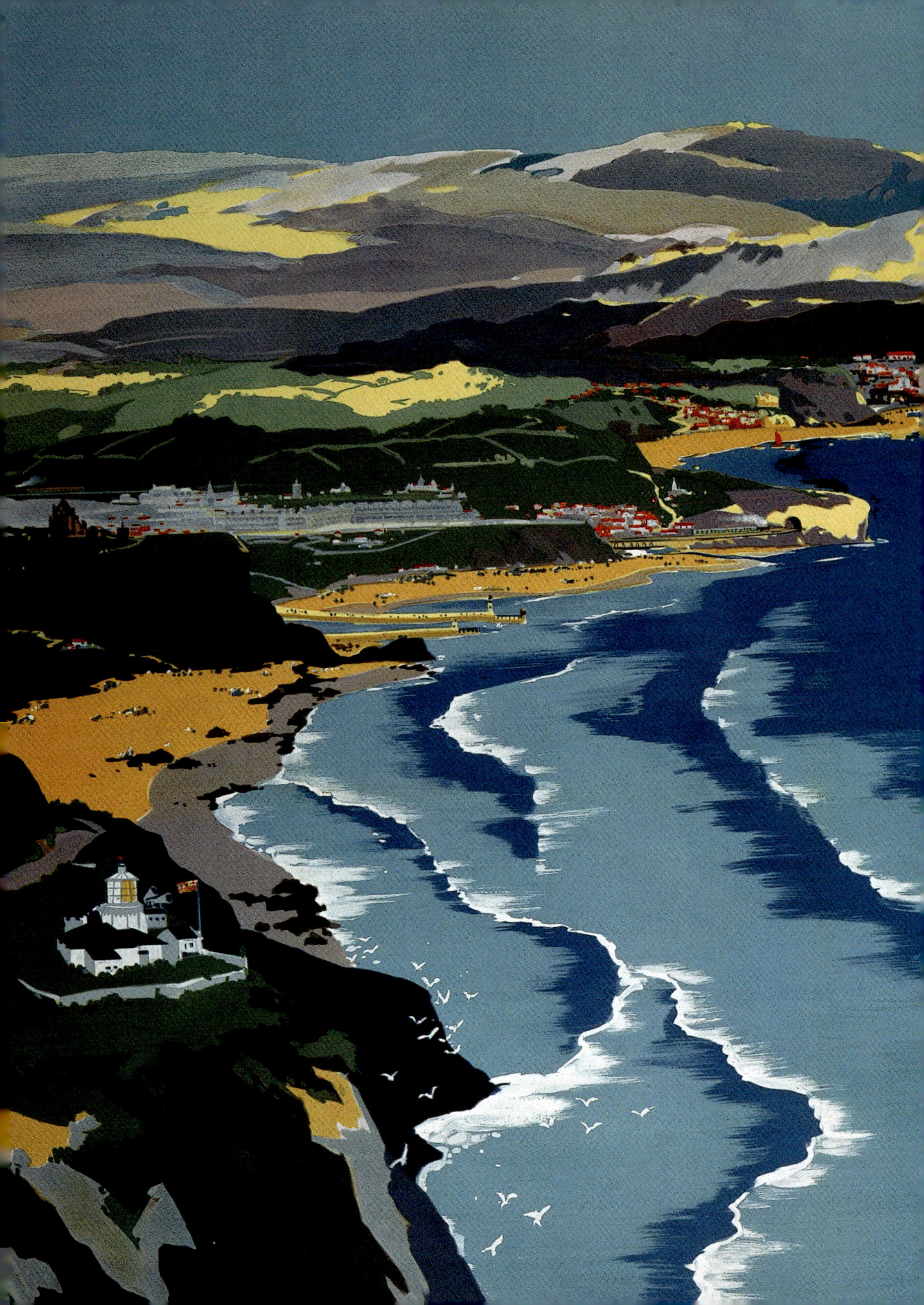

JULY

WEEK 27

MONDAY 3
FIRST QUARTER

TUESDAY 4
Holiday, USA (Independence Day)

WEDNESDAY 5

THURSDAY 6

FRIDAY 7

SATURDAY 8

SUNDAY 9

A poster by Frank Henry Mason, c.1938, produced for the LNER to promote holiday rail travel to the east coast of England.

WEEK 28

JULY

10 MONDAY

11 TUESDAY
FULL MOON

12 WEDNESDAY
Holiday, Northern Ireland (Battle of the Boyne)

13 THURSDAY

14 FRIDAY

15 SATURDAY
St Swithin's Day

16 SUNDAY

A BR poster by Alan Durman, 1952.

ICES
MINERALS
FILMS
FANCY
GOODS
HASTINGS
& ST. LEONARDS
Fine all the year round
FREQUENT FAST TRAINS
FROM LONDON (Victoria & Charing X)
BRITISH RAILWAYS
THROUGH TRAINS FROM
THE NORTH & MIDLANDS

Norman Wilkinson

JULY

WEEK 29

MONDAY 17
LAST QUARTER

TUESDAY 18

WEDNESDAY 19

THURSDAY 20

FRIDAY 21

SATURDAY 22

SUNDAY 23

Anglesey by Norman Wilkinson promoted travel by the LMS to Amlwch and Bull Bay on the Welsh island.

WEEK 30 | JULY

24 MONDAY

25 TUESDAY
NEW MOON

26 WEDNESDAY

27 THURSDAY

28 FRIDAY

29 SATURDAY

30 SUNDAY

An LNER poster by Graham Simmons promoting rail travel to the Scottish resort of Dunbar.

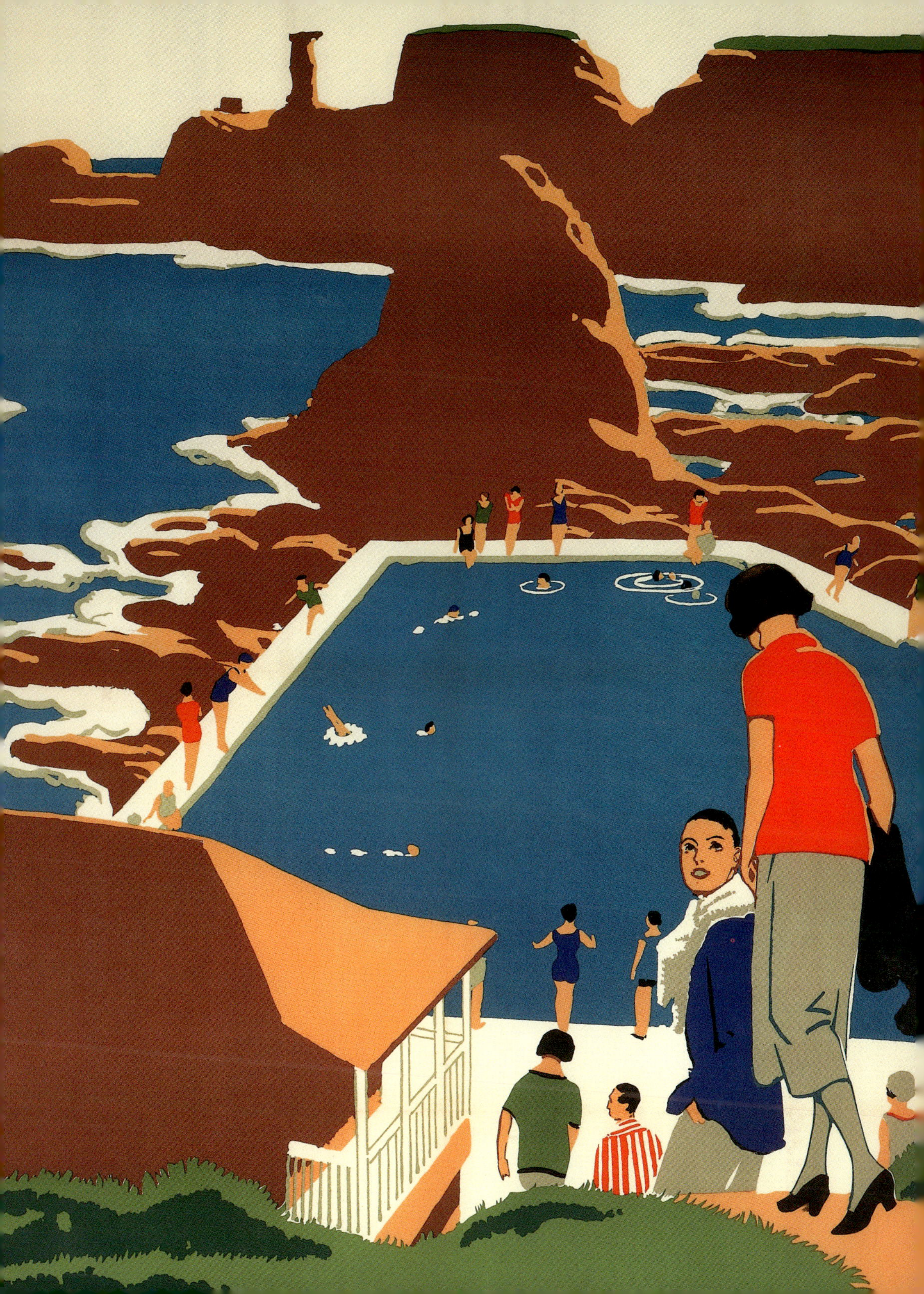

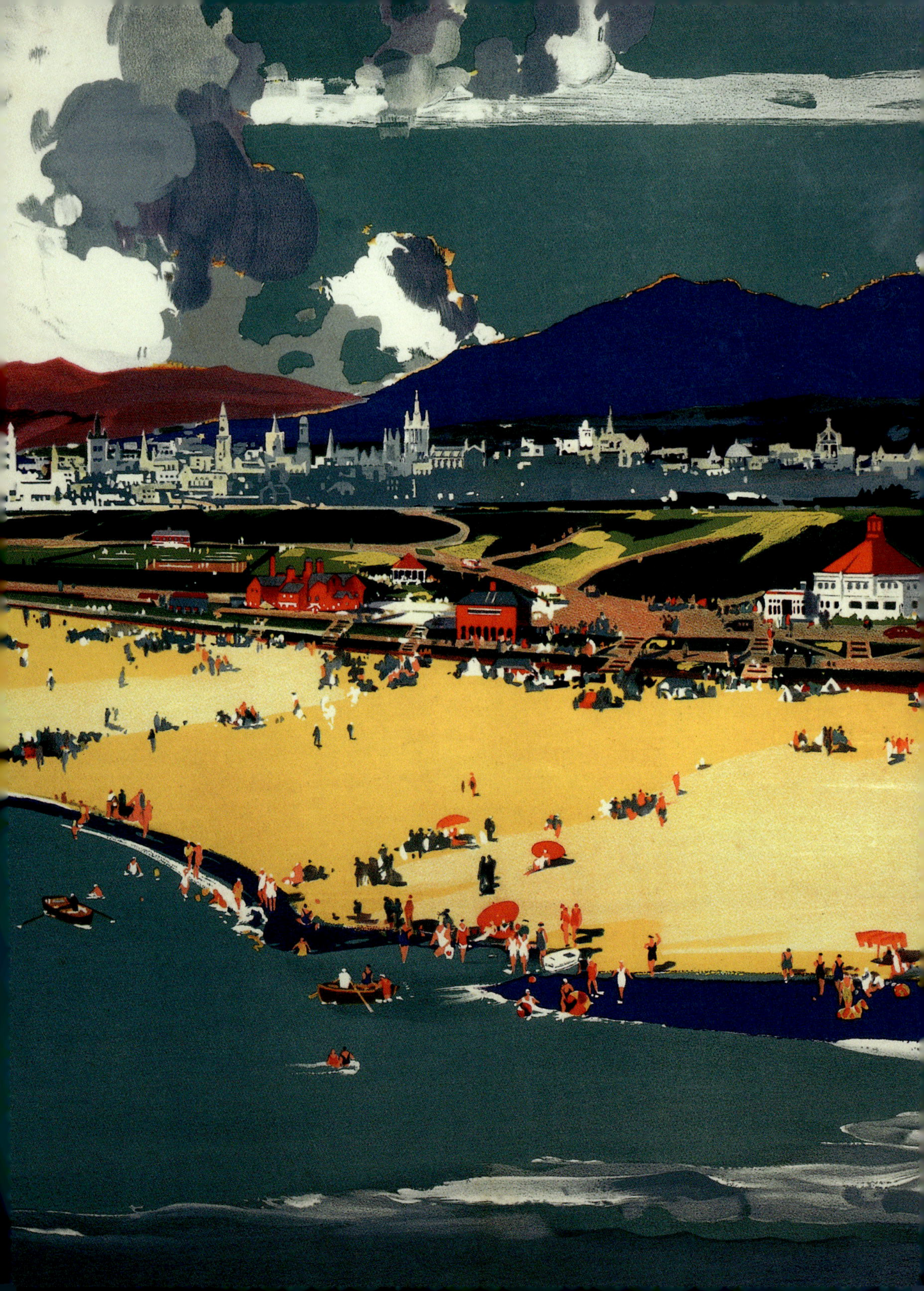

JULY & AUGUST

WEEK 31

MONDAY 31

TUESDAY 1

WEDNESDAY 2
FIRST QUARTER

THURSDAY 3

FRIDAY 4

SATURDAY 5

SUNDAY 6

The Silver City by the Sea by Frank Henry Mason, 1935, illustrating a poster produced jointly by the LNER and LMS, who advertised Aberdeen as the 'gateway to Royal Deeside'.

WEEK 32

AUGUST

7 MONDAY
Summer Bank Holiday, Scotland and Republic of Ireland

8 TUESDAY

9 WEDNESDAY
FULL MOON

10 THURSDAY

11 FRIDAY

12 SATURDAY

13 SUNDAY

An LNER poster of 1939 advertising stationary train carriages for hire as camping holiday accommodation.

L·N·E·R CAMPING COACHES
in England and Scotland

Accommodation for six persons from £2·10·0 per week
Ask for details at any L·N·E·R Station or Office

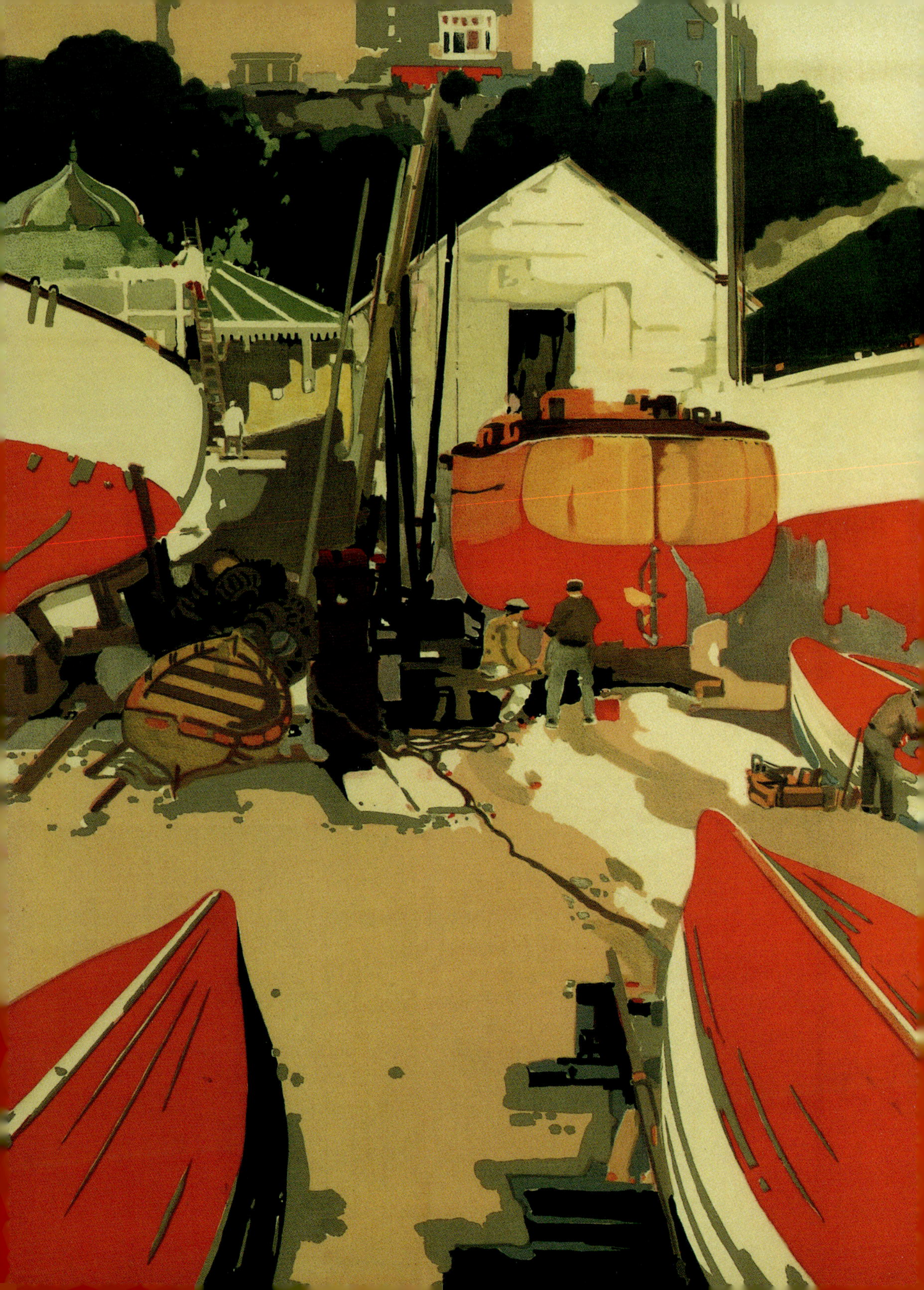

AUGUST

WEEK 33

MONDAY 14

TUESDAY 15

WEDNESDAY 16
LAST QUARTER

THURSDAY 17

FRIDAY 18

SATURDAY 19

SUNDAY 20

Getting Ready on the East Coast by Frank Henry Mason, produced by the LNER to promote rail travel to the east coast of England.

WEEK 34

AUGUST

21 MONDAY

22 TUESDAY

23 WEDNESDAY
NEW MOON

24 THURSDAY

25 FRIDAY

26 SATURDAY

27 SUNDAY

Portrush, 1952, a poster by Lance Cattermole advertising BR (London Midland Region) services to Portrush in Northern Ireland.

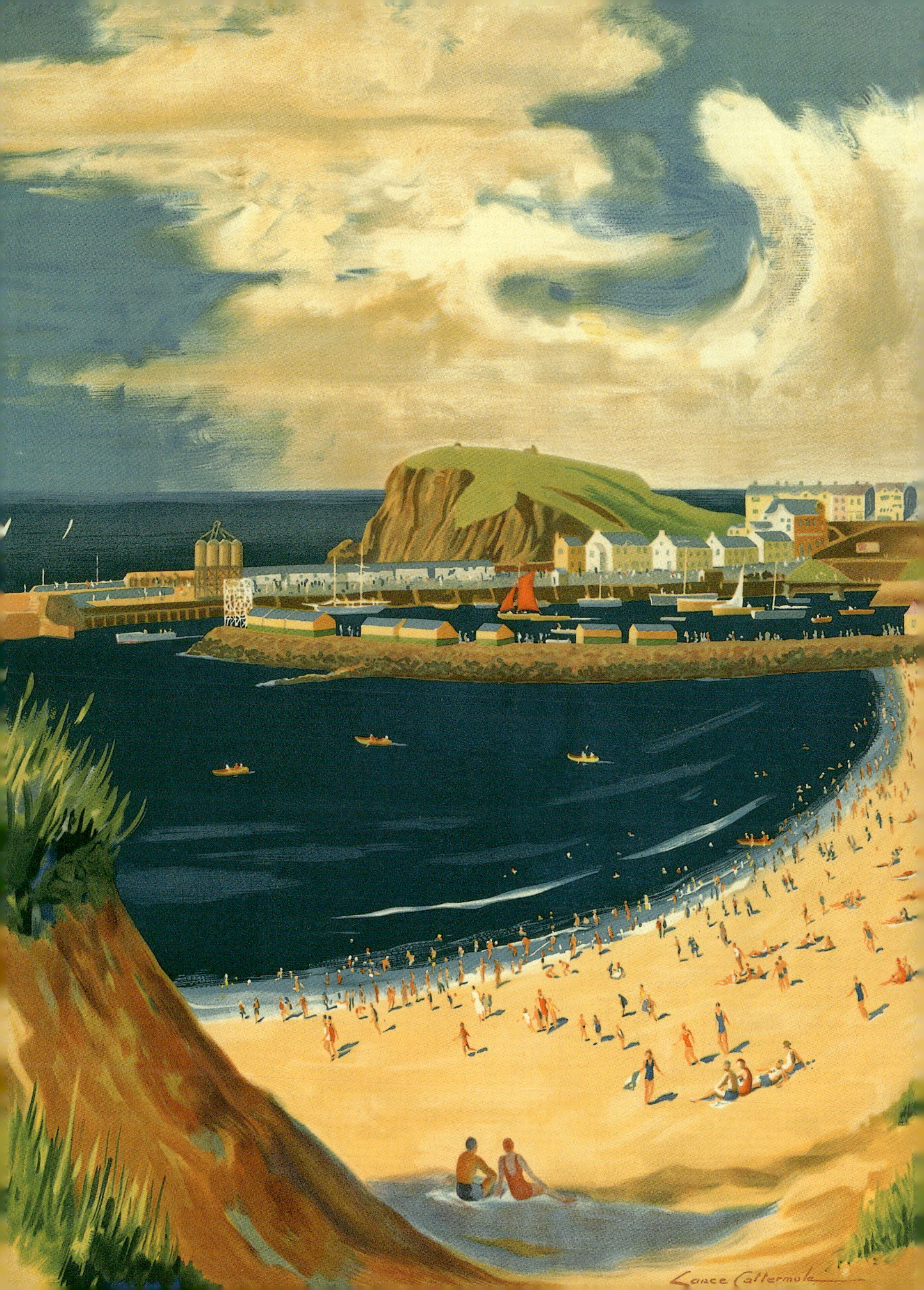
Lance Cattermole

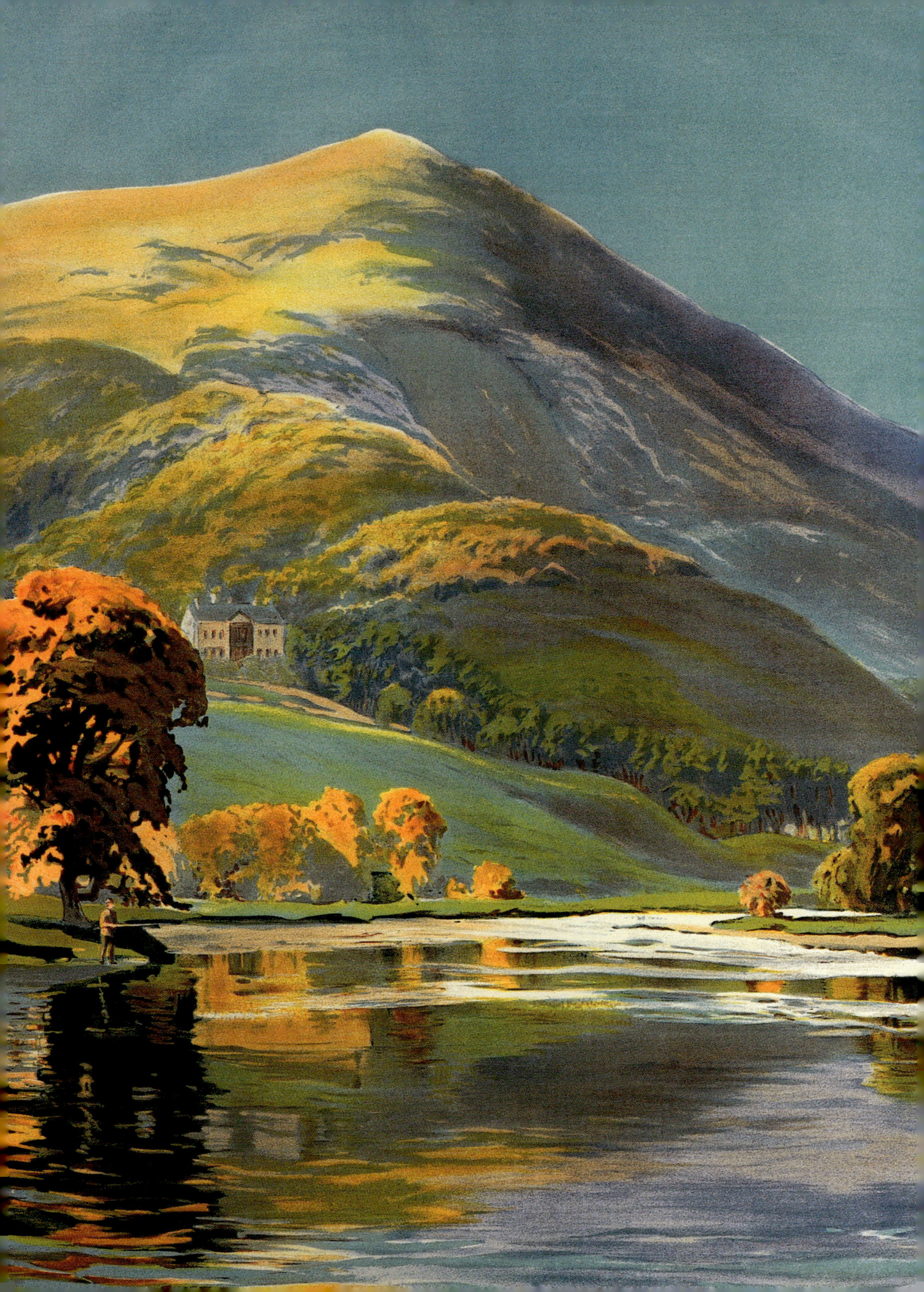

AUGUST & SEPTEMBER

WEEK 35

MONDAY **28**
Summer Bank Holiday, UK (exc. Scotland)

TUESDAY **29**

WEDNESDAY **30**

THURSDAY **31**
FIRST QUARTER

FRIDAY **1**

SATURDAY **2**

SUNDAY **3**
Father's Day, Australia and New Zealand

An LNER poster of the 1930s by A.G. Petherbridge advertising 'North Wales for scenery'.

WEEK 36

SEPTEMBER

4 MONDAY
Holiday, Canada (Labour Day) and USA (Labor Day)

5 TUESDAY

6 WEDNESDAY

7 THURSDAY
FULL MOON

8 FRIDAY

9 SATURDAY

10 SUNDAY

Saltburn by the Sea by Henry George Gawthorn, an LNER poster promoting rail travel to Saltburn-by-the-Sea, Redcar and Cleveland on the north-east coast of England.

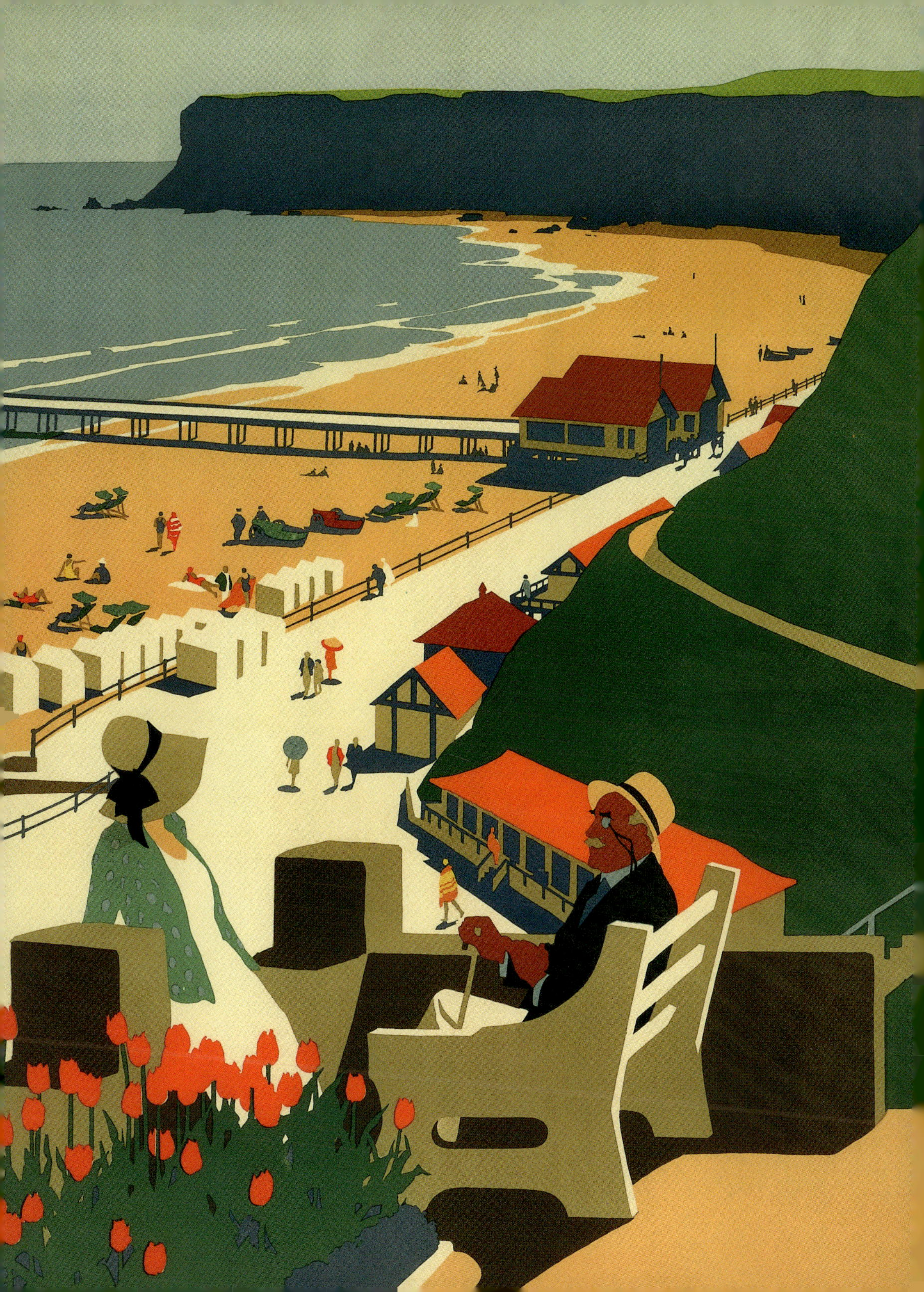

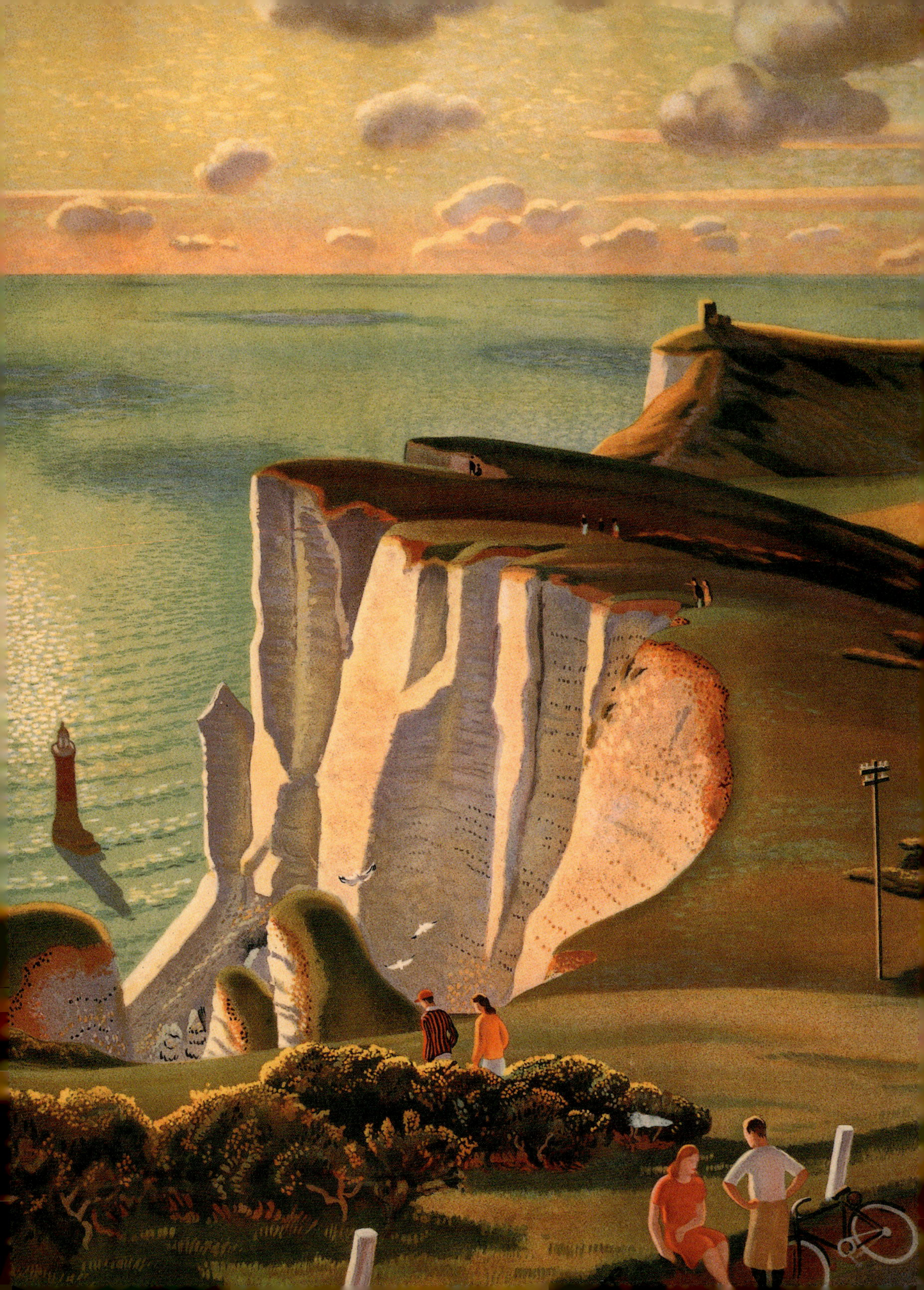

SEPTEMBER

WEEK 37

MONDAY **11**

TUESDAY **12**

WEDNESDAY **13**

THURSDAY **14**
LAST QUARTER

FRIDAY **15**

SATURDAY **16**

SUNDAY **17**

Downland Rambles by Adrian Allinson, a poster showing a panoramic view of the cliffs of Beachy Head, near Eastbourne. It was produced for BR in the 1950s to promote rail services to the East Sussex coast.

WEEK 38

SEPTEMBER

18 MONDAY

19 TUESDAY

20 WEDNESDAY

21 THURSDAY

22 FRIDAY
NEW MOON

23 SATURDAY
Autumnal Equinox
Jewish New Year (Rosh Hashanah)

24 SUNDAY
First Day of Ramadân (subject to sighting of the moon)

The Broads, 1932, by Robert Bartlett, a poster promoting LNER services to Norfolk.

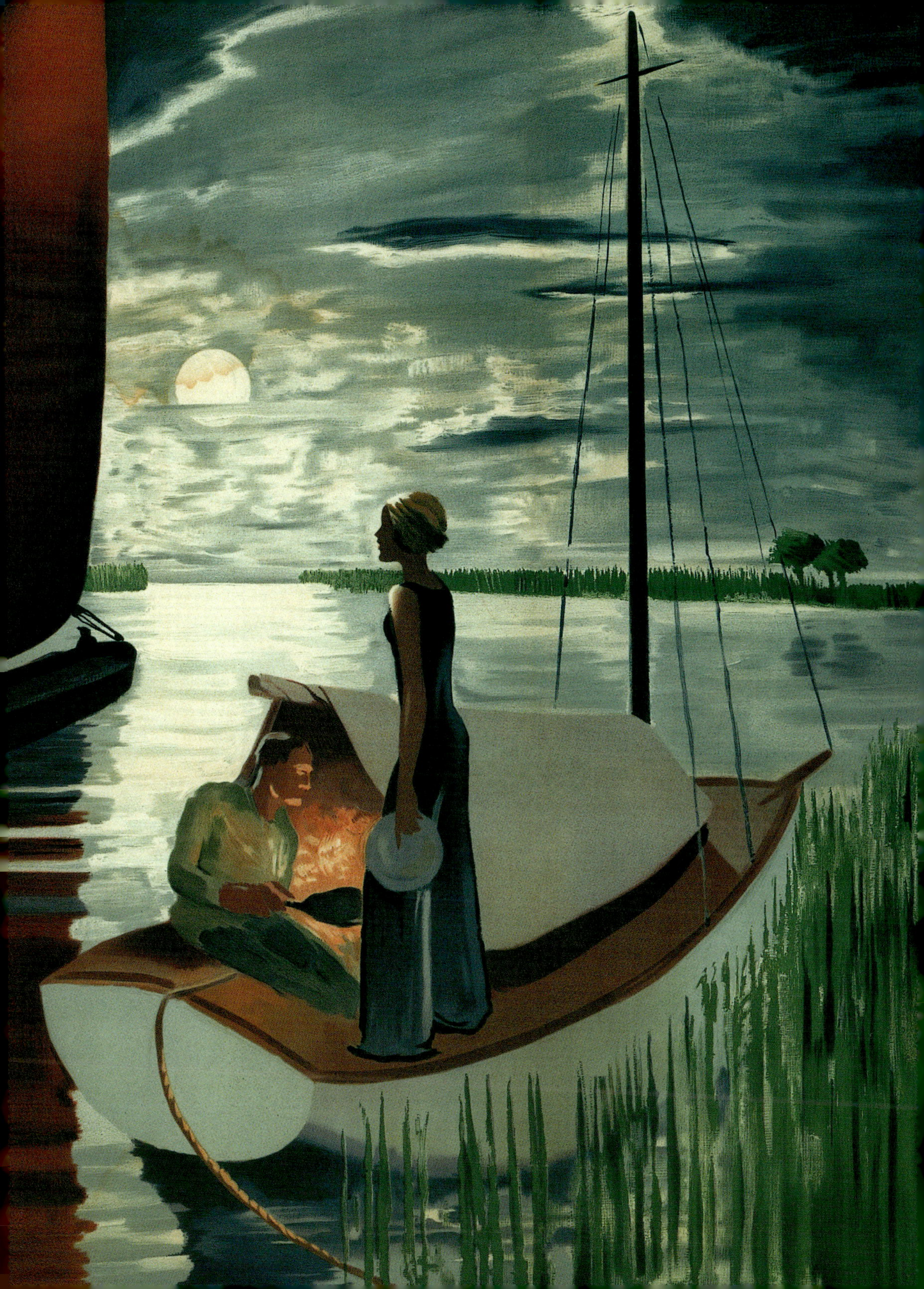

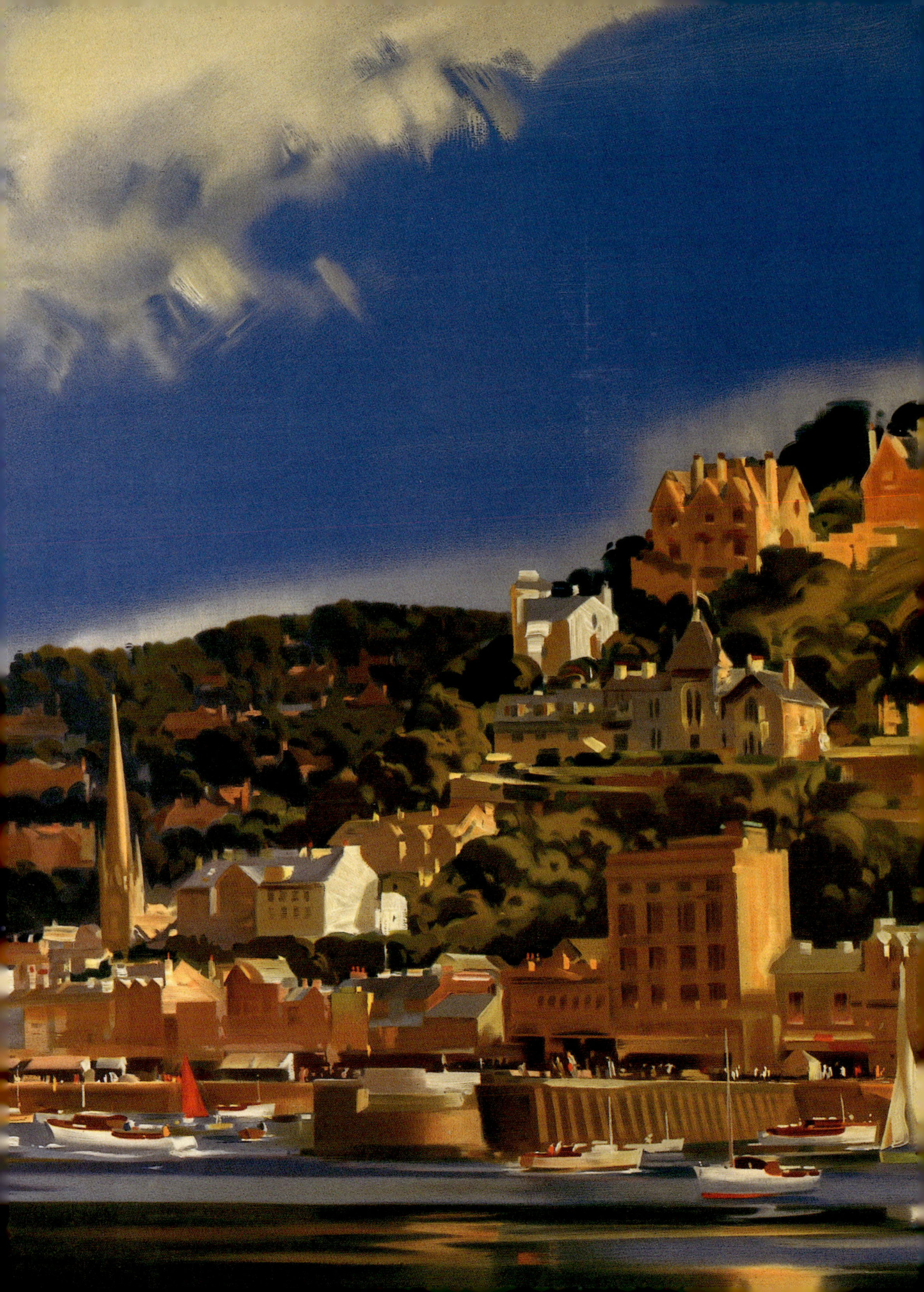

SEPTEMBER & OCTOBER

WEEK 39

MONDAY 25

TUESDAY 26

WEDNESDAY 27

THURSDAY 28

FRIDAY 29
Michaelmas Day

SATURDAY 30
FIRST QUARTER

SUNDAY 1

Torquay in Glorious Devon by Frank Wootton, a BR poster of the 1950s.

WEEK 40

OCTOBER

2 MONDAY
Jewish Day of Atonement (Yom Kippur)

3 TUESDAY

4 WEDNESDAY

5 THURSDAY

6 FRIDAY

7 SATURDAY
Jewish Festival of Tabernacles (Succoth), First Day
FULL MOON

8 SUNDAY

An LMS poster of the 1930s by Leonard Richmond promoting Bournemouth in Dorset as 'the centre of health and pleasure'.

BOURNEMOUTH

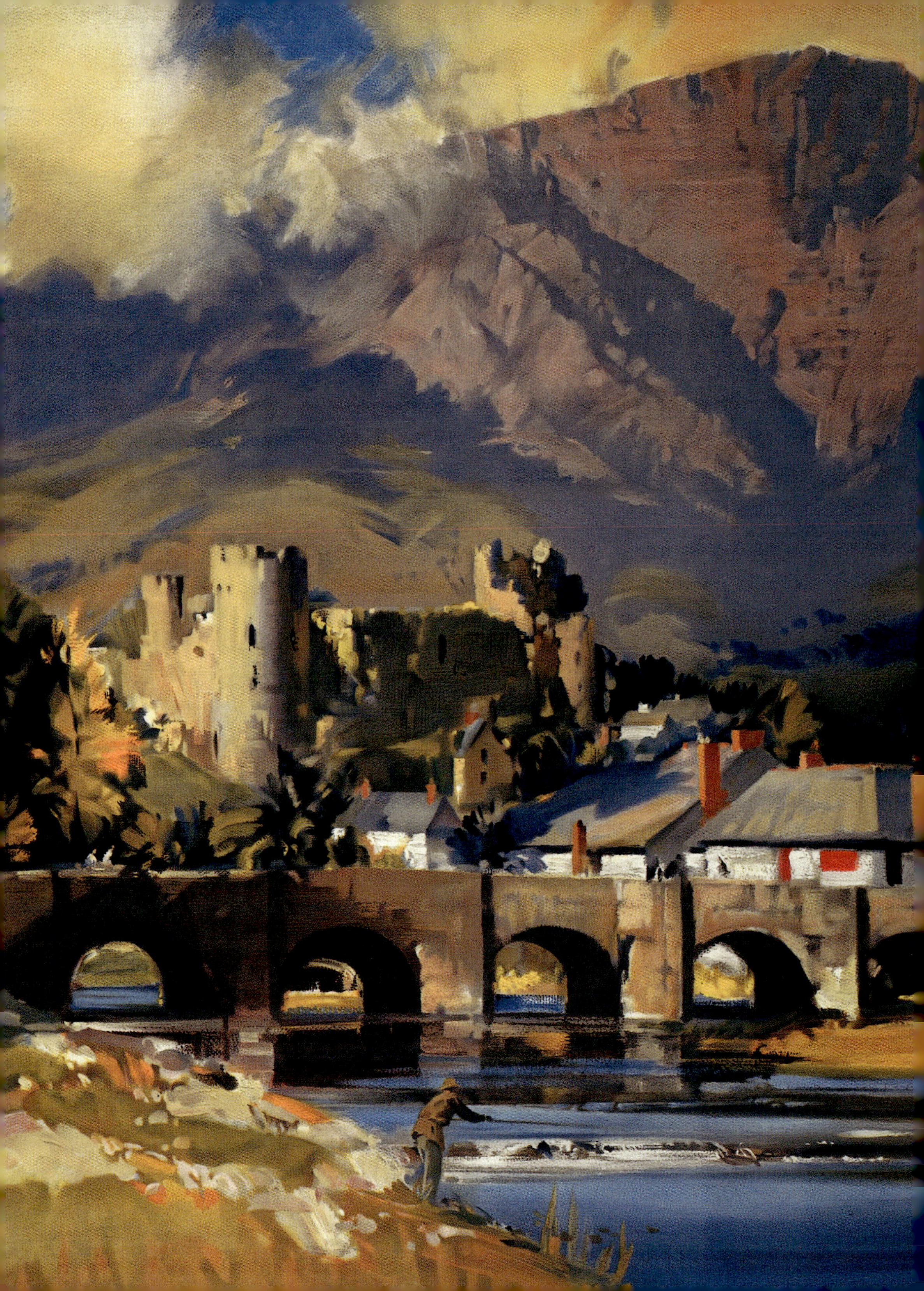

OCTOBER

WEEK 41

MONDAY **9**
Holiday, Canada (Thanksgiving Day)
Holiday, USA (Columbus Day)

TUESDAY **10**

WEDNESDAY **11**

THURSDAY **12**

FRIDAY **13**

SATURDAY **14**
Jewish Festival of Tabernacles (Succoth), Eighth Day
LAST QUARTER

SUNDAY **15**

A 1950s BR (Western Region) poster by Frank Wootton promoting rail travel to Wales.

WEEK 42

OCTOBER

16 MONDAY

17 TUESDAY

18 WEDNESDAY

19 THURSDAY

20 FRIDAY

21 SATURDAY

22 SUNDAY
NEW MOON

Compton Castle by Jack Merriott, a poster produced by BR (Western Region) to advertise rail services to Devon.

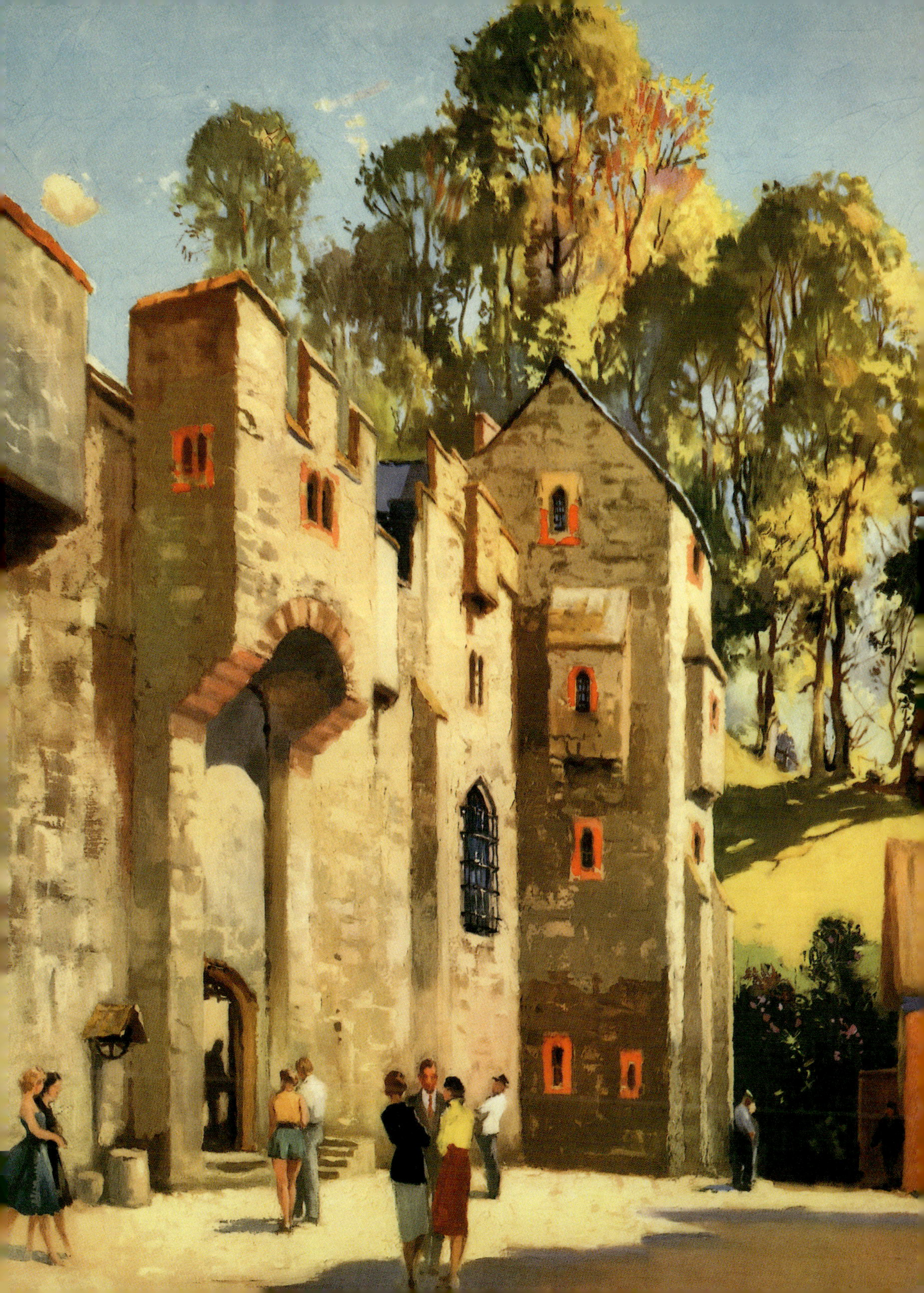

Ullswater.

OCTOBER

WEEK 43

MONDAY 23
Holiday, New Zealand (Labour Day)

TUESDAY 24
United Nations Day

WEDNESDAY 25

THURSDAY 26

FRIDAY 27

SATURDAY 28

SUNDAY 29
British Summertime ends
FIRST QUARTER

John Littlejohns' painting of Ullswater advertised 'English Lake-land' in Cumbria for the LNER.

WEEK 44   OCTOBER & NOVEMBER

30 MONDAY
Holiday, Republic of Ireland

31 TUESDAY
Hallowe'en

1 WEDNESDAY
All Saints' Day

2 THURSDAY

3 FRIDAY

4 SATURDAY

5 SUNDAY
Guy Fawkes' Day
FULL MOON

A poster by David Cobb advertising 'Northern Ireland – where the Mountains of Mourne sweep down to the sea', produced by BR (London Midland Region) in 1954.

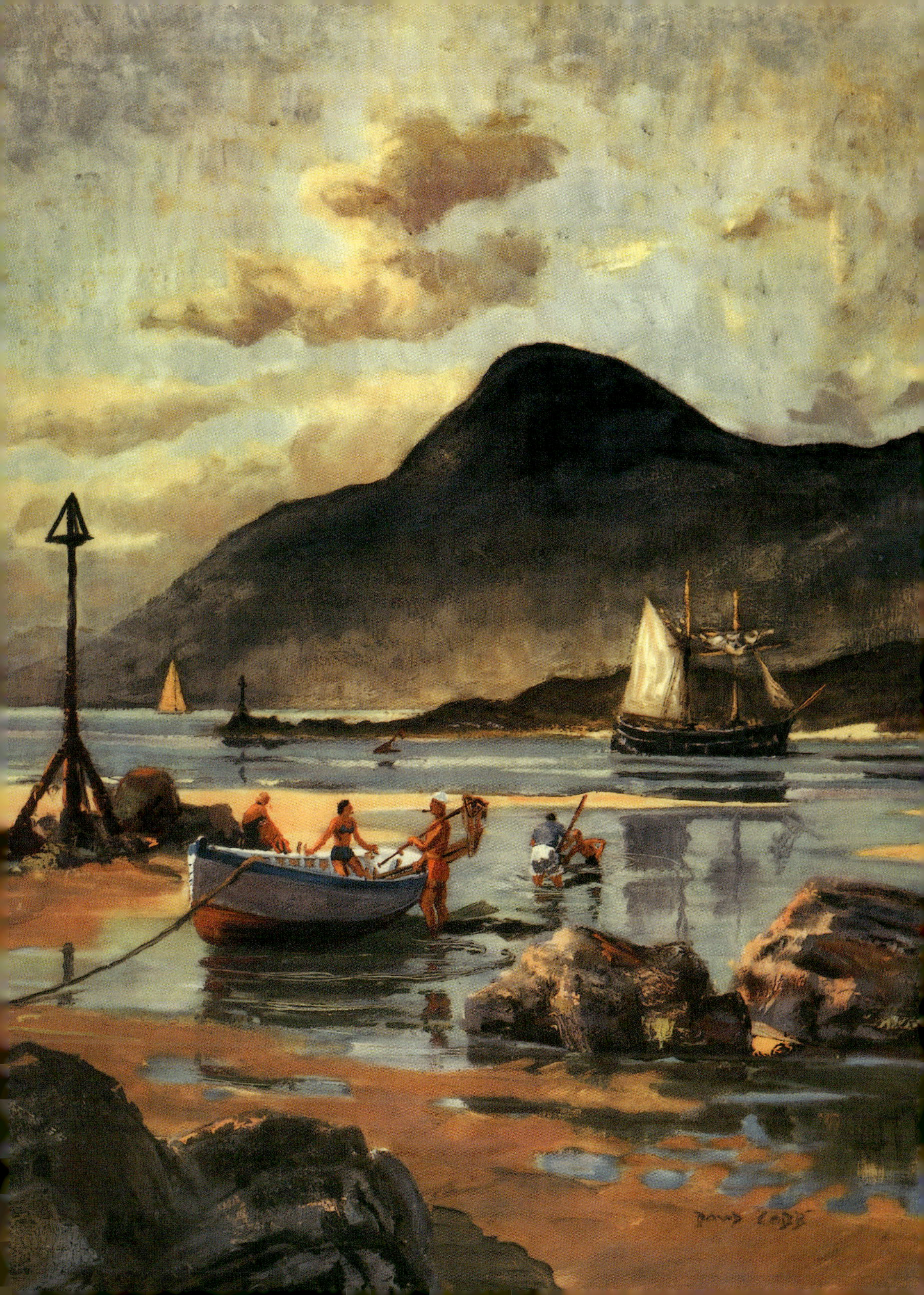

LNER

EPPING FOREST
QUICKLY REACHED FROM
LIVERPOOL STREET

NOVEMBER

WEEK 45

MONDAY **6**

TUESDAY **7**

WEDNESDAY **8**

THURSDAY **9**

FRIDAY **10**

SATURDAY **11**
Holiday, Canada (Remembrance Day) and USA (Veterans' Day)

SUNDAY **12**
Remembrance Sunday, UK
LAST QUARTER

An LNER poster advertising Epping Forest in Essex, by F. Gregory Brown.

WEEK 46

NOVEMBER

13 MONDAY

14 TUESDAY

15 WEDNESDAY

16 THURSDAY

17 FRIDAY

18 SATURDAY

19 SUNDAY

Staffordshire Potteries, 1923, an LMS poster by Norman Wilkinson.

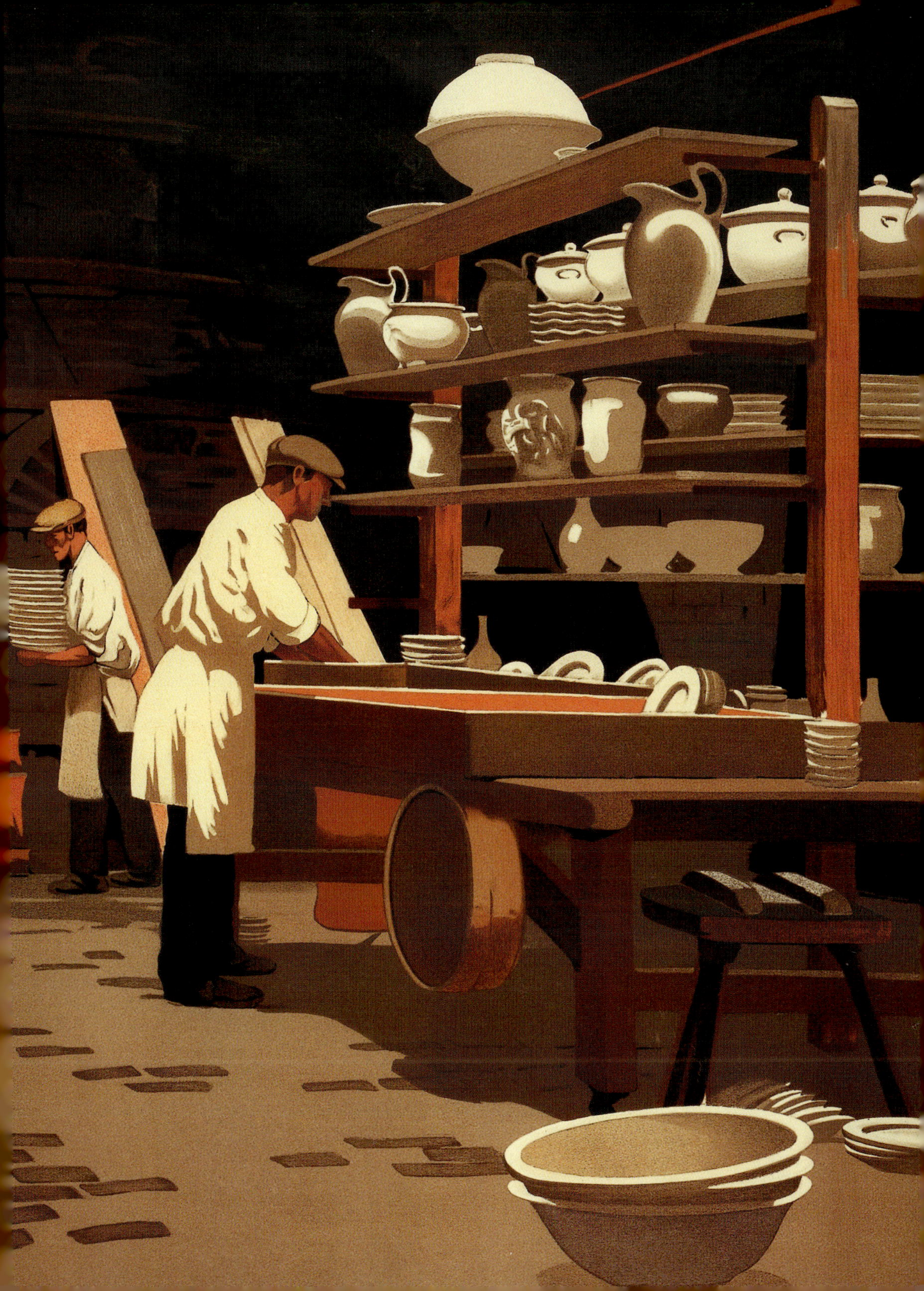

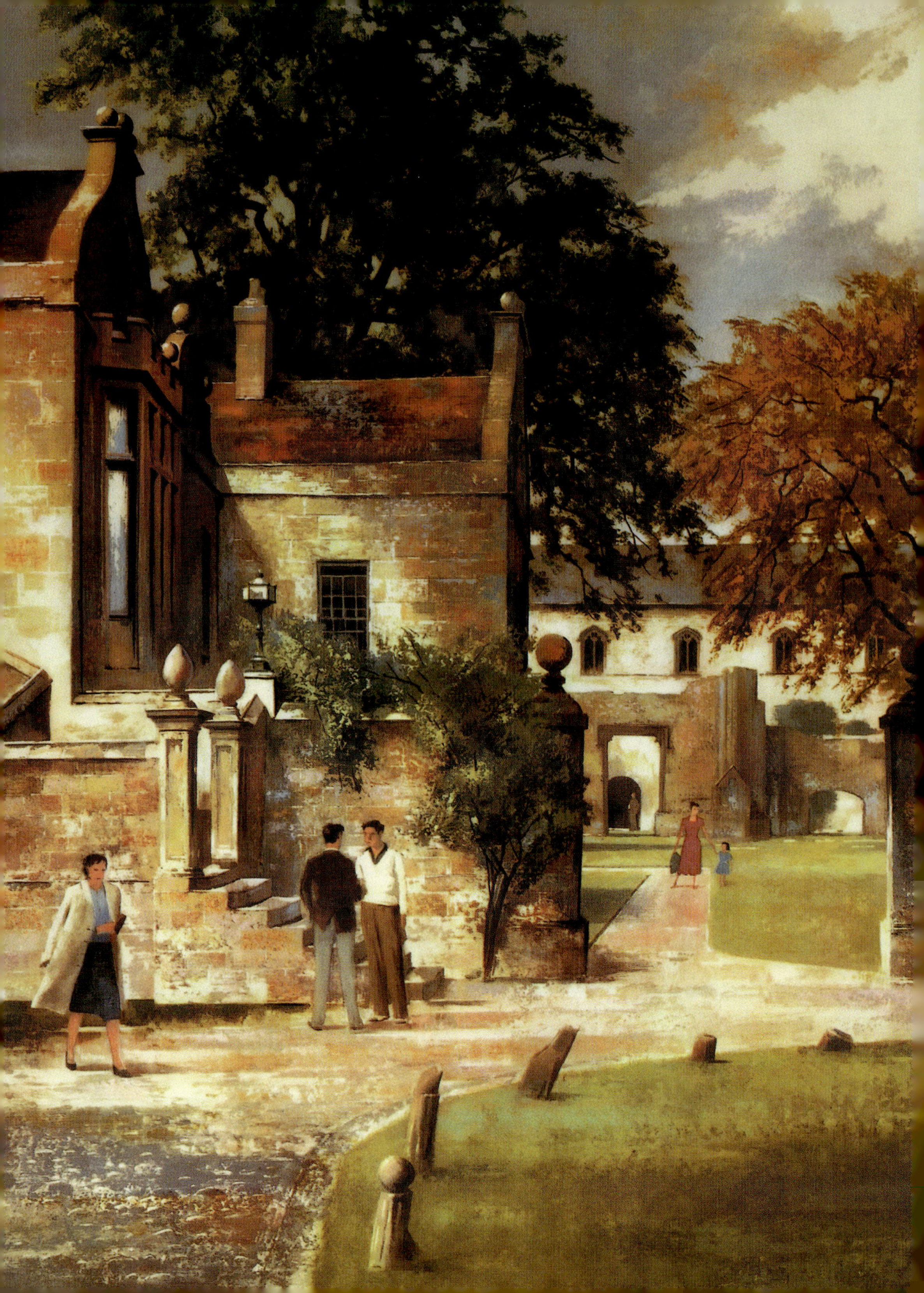

NOVEMBER

WEEK 47

MONDAY 20
NEW MOON

TUESDAY 21

WEDNESDAY 22

THURSDAY 23
Holiday, USA (Thanksgiving Day)

FRIDAY 24

SATURDAY 25

SUNDAY 26

A 1959 BR (London Midland Region) poster by John Greene showing Whalley Abbey in Lancashire.

WEEK 48

NOVEMBER & DECEMBER

27 MONDAY

28 TUESDAY
FIRST QUARTER

29 WEDNESDAY

30 THURSDAY
St Andrew's Day

1 FRIDAY

2 SATURDAY

3 SUNDAY
Advent Sunday

The Pass of Aberglaslyn, Gwynedd, North Wales, 1945, by Norman Wilkinson: an LMS poster.

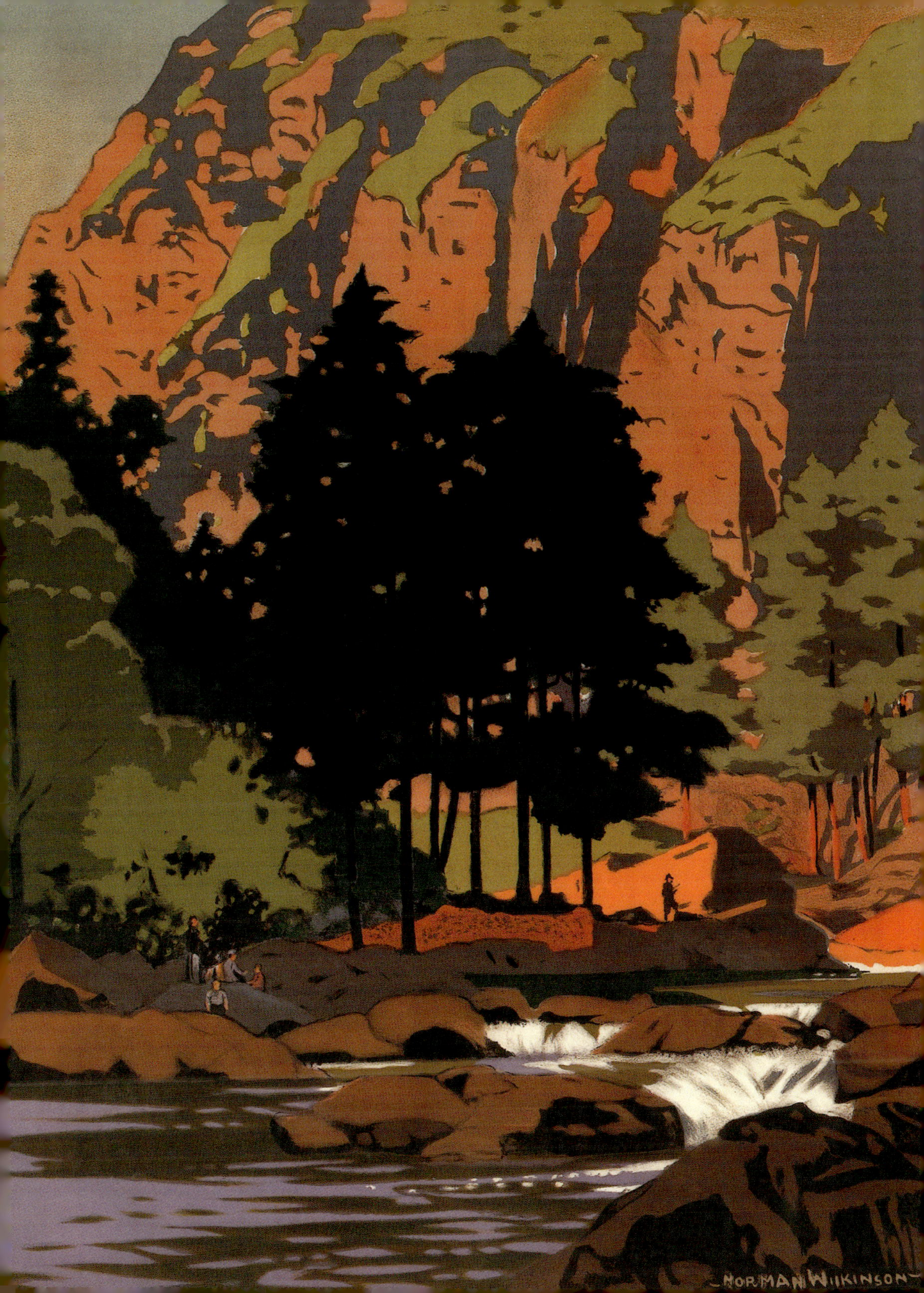
NORMAN WILKINSON

RAMBLES ON THE
YORKSHIRE COAST AND MOORS

DECEMBER

WEEK 49

MONDAY 4

TUESDAY 5
FULL MOON

WEDNESDAY 6

THURSDAY 7

FRIDAY 8

SATURDAY 9

SUNDAY 10

The Bridestone by Schabelsky, an LNER poster.

WEEK 50

DECEMBER

11 MONDAY

12 TUESDAY
LAST QUARTER

13 WEDNESDAY

14 THURSDAY

15 FRIDAY

16 SATURDAY
Jewish Festival of Chanukah, First Day

17 SUNDAY

With the slogan 'Harrogate: come for health, stay for pleasure' and Fred Taylor's illustration of the auditorium of the Royal Hall, the LNER advertised its services to the Yorkshire town in 1930.

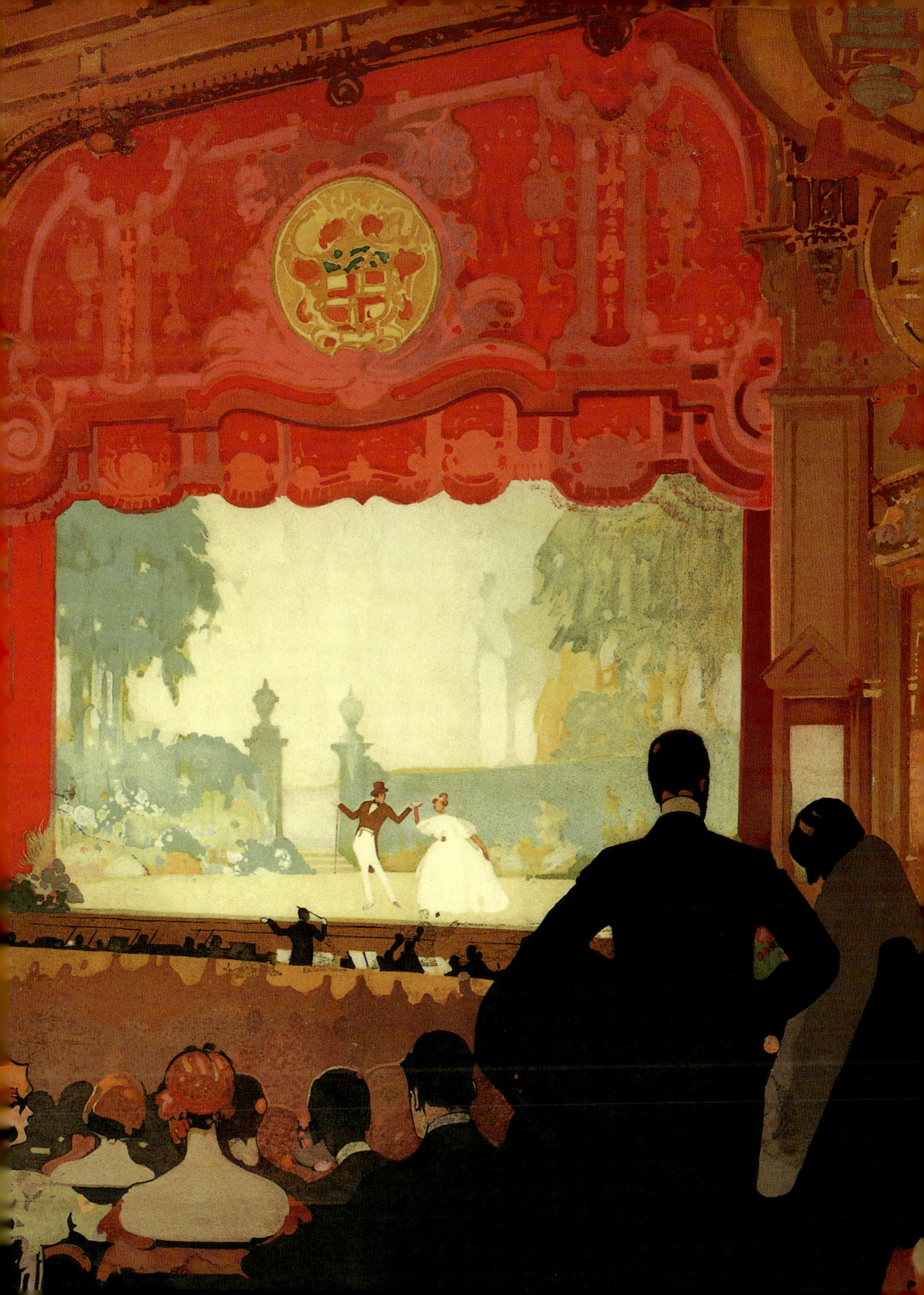

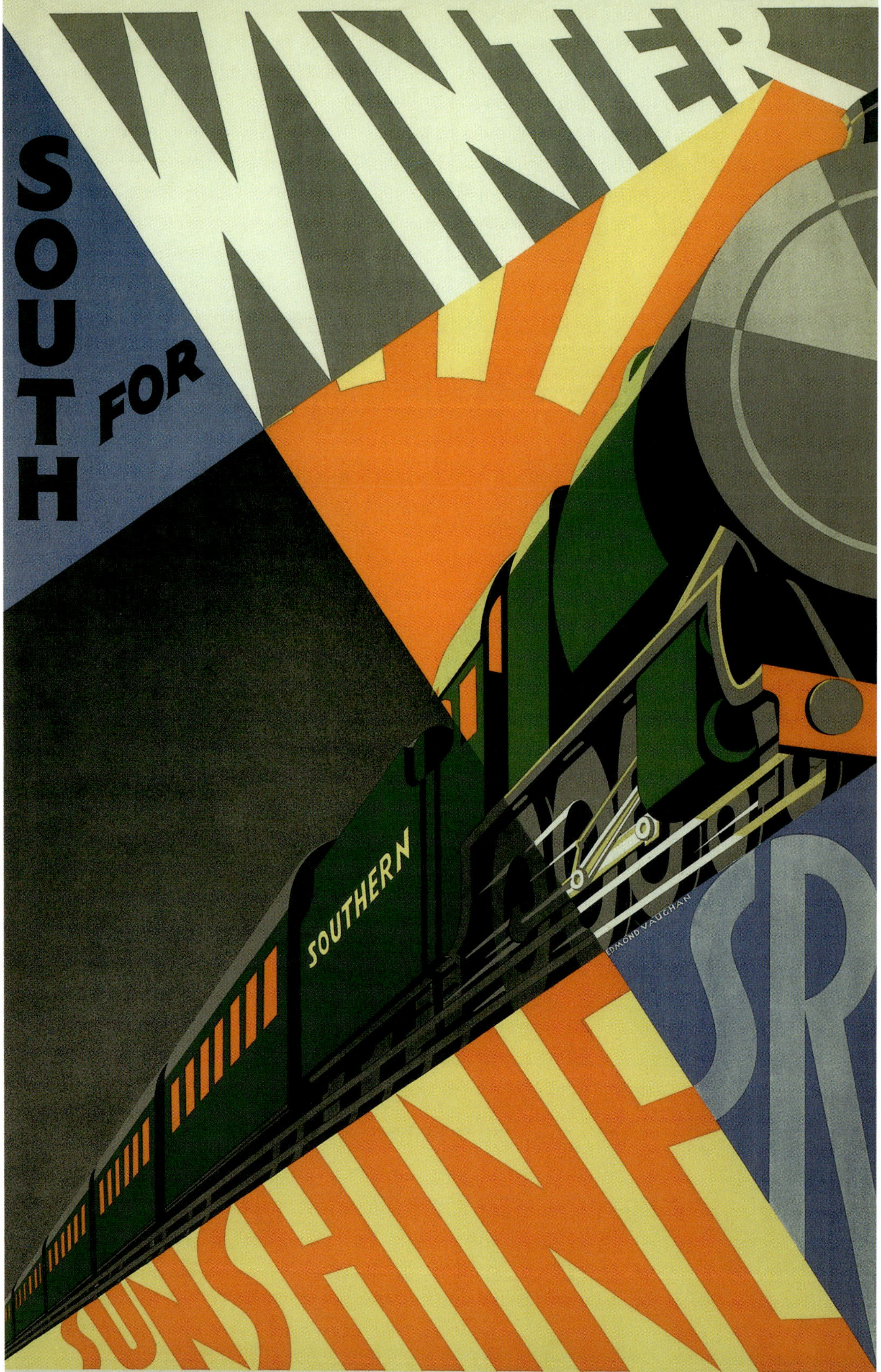
SOUTH FOR
WINTER
SUNSHINE
SOUTHERN
EDMOND VAUGHAN
SR

DECEMBER

WEEK 51

MONDAY **18**

TUESDAY **19**

WEDNESDAY **20**
NEW MOON

THURSDAY **21**

FRIDAY **22**
Winter Solstice

SATURDAY **23**

SUNDAY **24**
Christmas Eve

This SR poster by Edmond Vaughan advertised the south of England as a sunny destination for winter holidays in 1929.

WEEK 52

DECEMBER

25 MONDAY
Christmas Day
Holiday, UK, Republic of Ireland,
Canada, USA, Australia and New Zealand

26 TUESDAY
Boxing Day (St Stephen's Day)
Holiday, UK, Republic of Ireland,
Canada, Australia and New Zealand

27 WEDNESDAY
FIRST QUARTER

28 THURSDAY

29 FRIDAY

30 SATURDAY

31 SUNDAY
New Year's Eve

The LNER produced this poster by C.R.W. Nevinson in 1925 to promote rail services to the British Empire Exhibition at Wembley, London.

NOTES